Drink, Play, F@#k

Drink, Play, F@#k

One Man's Search for Anything Across Ireland, Vegas, and Thailand

ANDREW GOTTLIEB

Black Cat
a paperback original imprint of Grove/Atlantic, Inc.
New York

Published simultaneously in Canada
Printed in the United States of America

FIRST EDITION

ISBN-10: 0-8021-7052-8
ISBN-13: 978-0-8021-7052-1

Black Cat
a paperback original imprint of Grove/Atlantic, Inc.
841 Broadway
New York, NY 10003

Distributed by Publishers Group West

www.groveatlantic.com

09 10 11 12   10 9 8 7 6 5 4 3 2 1

For the real Alicia

Truth is mighty and will prevail. There is nothing the matter with this, except that it ain't so.★

——Mark Twain

★I have no idea what this means.

O

or

Introduction

or

How This Book Works

or

The Thirty-seventh and Thirty-eighth Numbers

The seventeenth-century French mathematician Blaise Pascal is one of those guys who kind of almost invented everything way before everyone else did, only he didn't. Computers, the flush toilet, the wristwatch . . . Pascal just missed nailing all of these marvelous contributions to modern society. He was on the right track but never quite made it to the station. Aside from a bunch of theorems and triangles and stuff, his greatest real invention was the result of another failure. While unsuccessfully trying to come up with a perpetual motion machine, Pascal accidentally created the roulette wheel—a brilliant contraption featuring thirty-six numbers and thirty-six ways to make a fortune or to lose all of your money.

At hundreds of casinos from Reno, Nevada, to Atmore, Alabama, to Coconut Creek, Florida, you can hit the tables, put down a bet on any one of those numbers, and get paid off to the tune of thirty-five to one. If you found a spot where the limits were high enough, you could turn $6,250 into $218,750 in a few seconds just because your Little League number was seventeen and you woke up with a lucky feeling.

I've spent a lot of time in casinos recently and I can tell you firsthand that there is almost no better feeling—and I'm factoring in sex, drugs, sports, rage, alcohol, love, dessert, linen sheets, fresh fruit, and religion—than hitting your number at roulette. I can also tell you that getting wiped out at the table feels like getting nut punched by an angry biker with enormous fists.

I didn't used to have this kind of sophisticated perspective about the gambling arts. My name is Bob Sullivan,[1] and I used to be just another overpaid account executive logging hour after hour at a large Manhattan ad agency while trundling my way through a life of comfort, expectation, and—let's face it—boredom. The boredom pretty much stopped, however, when my wife of eight years decided to leave me for another man while vociferously suffering the mother of all existential crises. Some might suggest that these events led to a crisis of my own.

Maybe I'm going out on a limb here, but after everything I've been through—after all the heartache I've suffered and joy I've felt, after all the strange sights that I've seen, the bizarre

---

[1] "Bob Sullivan" is a pseudonym. All you Bob Sullivans out there, please don't sue me.

situations I've encountered, and the weird and fascinating people whom I've met—I've come to one simple conclusion: life is not just like roulette, life *is* roulette. And, since this book is about life—or at least one year in my life—I've decided to organize it like a roulette wheel with thirty-six chapters describing the year I spent out there. "Out there" in this case being a euphemism for "anywhere where I could get away from the unrelenting heartache caused by my wife suddenly stabbing me in the back."

I'm also going to include two extra chapters to represent the two numbers added over time to Pascal's roulette wheel, 0 and 00. 0 and 00 are sneaky bastards. When they hit, it always comes as a surprise—as if someone snuck those evil green digits onto the wheel while it was spinning too fast to notice. And when they hit it usually leads to that brutal nut punch I mentioned earlier.

The three sections of this book will each focus on one of the locations in which I spent the year in question, desperately trying to get my head and heart together after my wife had so enthusiastically poured battery acid over both of them. From the pubs of Ireland, to the casinos of Las Vegas, to the hedonistic pleasure palaces of Thailand, I learned a great deal during my twelve months of isolation, degradation, depredation, inebriation, confabulation, masturbation, consternation, and elation. One of the most important lessons that I learned was not to fear the zeroes. Yes, they're unfair. And, yes, they reduce the odds of winning and add to the house's already hefty advantage. But they also make things fun. The great victories in life are never sure things. Anyone can beat up a toddler—especially if he's napping. But when Buster Douglas dropped Mike Tyson that cold February night in Tokyo, he made history. He also paid out at forty-two to one.

I am a simple man. I believe in only a few things, but I learned these things the hard way so I believe in them absolutely. I don't consider myself a spiritual person. Either I've been too busy to think about that stuff or it just felt stupid to do so. But I'll tell you one thing that I really do believe: If you listen to the roulette wheel, it will talk to you. And sometimes it will even whisper what number's about to hit.

0 0

or

The Second of Those Two Extra Chapters

or

Maybe This Roulette Analogy Isn't Working

I used to have a plan. It wasn't a brilliant blueprint designed by crafty German Bauhaus architects. It was a simple outline for how I wanted to live my life. And, without wanting to sound boastful, I think that it was a solid plan: have some fun while I'm young, work hard after college, meet a couple of ladies, marry one of them, make lots of money, drive an expensive car, have some kids, worry about my receding hairline, watch lots of sports on TV, die. A nice, basic plan, right? And everything was unfolding beautifully. I was in the middle of step six, blissfully unaware of the shitstorm that was heading my way, when the bottom fell out—of my marriage, that is. The expensive car held up nicely.

To be totally honest, there were problems with my plan even before my wife shoved a nuclear bomb down the pants of our life together. I might have spent too much time at the office. I probably could have met a few more ladies before marrying one of them. I definitely should have put my foot down about all the pasta-making courses, ballet recitals, and poetry readings she made me go to. And regular viewings of Shakespeare in the Park turned out not to solve the problems that already existed in my life. I really did love that car, though.

I'm pretty much through with planning now. See, I used to think of myself as just another guy watching that white ball bounce around, hoping it would land on my number. I felt that I wasn't in control of what was happening in my life and that made me nervous and anxious. But I've come to realize that I'm not some wide-eyed hopeful bellied up to the baize watching helplessly as a random white ball decides my fate. I now know that I'm not fully in control of what will happen to me, nor will I ever be. But that's okay. Because I also know that I'm not just watching the white ball, I *am* the white ball. And it doesn't matter where I land, because each number has something wonderful and magical to offer. Especially twenty-nine.

During my travels and travails through Ireland, Las Vegas, and Thailand, I met some amazing people. Some of them were amazing douche bags. Some became my guides. Some became my closest friends. And one of them became my own personal guru. Not in the way you're thinking. There was no yoga or incense or creepy bald dude in a unitard helping me realign my chakras. Rick was more like a teacher, or mentor, or guardian angel, or golf buddy, or whatever the hell you want to call him. Maybe guru was just a bad choice of word. After all, how many gurus sleep on the bathroom floor of the Twenty-third

Street YMCA and have actually beaten the Big Game at the Bellagio for a hundred grand?

I'm using Rick's real name, and the real names of several other important people whom I met while I was on the road. Some other names and locations have been fictionalized out of respect for people's privacy and my aforementioned desire not to be sued. Aside from that I've tried to relate everything exactly the way it happened—or at least the way I remembered it. And how much more can you realistically expect from a bouncing ceramic spheroid?

Book One

Ireland

or

"Drink deep, or taste not the Pierian Spring."
—Alexander Pope

or

12 Tales About Getting Wrecked

I

I wish Giovanna would kiss me.

There are many reasons why this would be a terrible idea. Giovanna is an exchange student from Milan studying marketing in Dublin. I am an American businessman in my late thirties hiding out in Ireland trying to get so drunk that my wife's recent betrayal will stop burning my insides like hot lava. Giovanna's a beautiful young Italian goddess with a lion's mane of jet-black hair, and I'm a thoroughly average-looking New Englander with the beginnings of love handles and some gray creeping into my temples. So Giovanna is almost twenty years younger than I am. She is engaged to a guy named Teodoro back in Italy. She is sweet, and innocent, and deeply religious. But the real reason why Giovanna kissing me would be a terrible idea is that she is so incredibly drunk right now that if she were to kiss me, she'd probably throw up all over my face.

Ireland is an amazing country. In no other spot that I have come across on my travels has drinking to excess been accepted to such a degree as normal, everyday behavior. I used to think that Texans didn't actually wear cowboy hats—that it was just a stereotype propagated by movies and TV. But one day I had a stopover in the Houston airport and I saw a bunch of people wearing cowboy hats for real in a totally nonironic fashion. Well, Ireland is just like that—only instead of cowboy hats, it's people getting shitfaced. And instead of just a handful of good ol' boys rocking their ten-gallon lids, it's every single person in the country slamming shot after shot and beer after beer from morning till night and then starting all over again.

As further proof that Ireland is committed to promoting a drinks-based culture, I'd like to point out that one of the most popular sections of Dublin, where all the tourists go and the fun happens, is called Temple Bar. They have the word "bar" in the name of their most famous neighborhood! That would be like Parisians calling the Latin Quarter the Escargot Quarter, or Los Angelenos changing the name from Beverly Hills to Cocaineville.

In defense of the Dubliners, the "bar" in Temple Bar doesn't actually refer to a bar where you order drinks. But it's not like they don't know about their international reputation for throwing it down. If the Irish didn't want to encourage the stereotype that they're all booze hounds, they easily could have called the place Old Dublin, or South Bank, or Liffeytown or something. But these sauceheads love everything that even tangentially has anything to do with alcohol. So they have been calling the cultural center of their capital city Temple Bar for four hundred years.

There's a reason that the Emerald Isle has never produced any world-class painters, sculptors, or architects—none of them could hold a brush, chisel, or pencil steady enough to get the job done. The poets could dash down their rhymes and romances in shaky letters on cocktail napkins in between pints. And the singers could wail and moan while teetering on the verge of alcoholic unconsciousness—but that's where Ireland's artistic contributions peter out. These people really drink, is my point. If you were to cut an Irish hemophiliac, you'd have beer on tap until the poor bastard bled out.

I should mention that as I'm staring at Giovanna's gorgeous face, lustrous hair, and devastating green eyes, I'm probably even drunker than she is. Here is a quick recap of what I've had to drink in the three hours leading up to my current emotional quandary: six pints of Guinness, six shots of Inishowen, three large Bacardi Breezers, two glasses of red wine, half a glass of water. At this point it's really a toss-up between Giovanna and me as to who is going to puke on whom first. But as I'm staring into those lovely, albeit significantly glazed-over green eyes, allow me to flash back to another occasion when I was staring into a woman's eyes. This time they are my wife's eyes—also green—but at the moment I'm remembering they are more red than green as she has been crying hysterically in the bathroom for about an hour.

2

There are approximately a dozen possible explanations as to why my wife might have been crying hysterically for about an hour. In ascending order of significance, these are some of the things that made her weep uncontrollably: world hunger, accidentally skipping breakfast, missing a sale at Barney's, not enough women on the Supreme Court, noticing a new frown line, political persecution in far-off lands, thinking she's not as pretty as her sister, the subway, anything having to do with me.

My guess is that this tear binge was primarily driven by the last option—but you never know. Once while we were staying at the Four Seasons Resort at Punta Mita, Mexico, she wouldn't leave the room for two days because she didn't want anyone to see the bags under her eyes that were a direct result of her sobbing about the possibility that she might have bags under her eyes. For those of you keeping score at home, the Four Seasons Resort at Punta Mita, Mexico, is a very expensive hotel. And having a profoundly neurotic, self-obsessed wife turns out not to be a valid excuse for a refund.

On the night in question, however, I just knew that this was all my fault—that *I* was the bags under her eyes. There was a familiarity to this wailing that I had dealt with many times in the past. I was getting the same vibe that I used to get when I'd forget about meaningless pseudo-anniversaries or when I didn't introduce her "quickly enough" to people at the office Christmas party.

As I lay in bed desperately trying to pretend that not only was I still asleep, but I was so deeply asleep that even loud caterwauling couldn't possibly wake me up, I wracked my brain to try and remember what I possibly could have done wrong. My checklist was pretty slim. I never cheated on her, I never hit her, I was nice to her family, I paid for all of her stuff. When you get right down to it—what else is a decent husband supposed to do?

The correct answer to that question is "not much." Her answer to that question was "a lot." I discovered this when she finally called my sleep bluff by storming out of the bathroom and making a caustic remark about my testicles. I believe that the exact phrase was, "You got some kind of balls!" At that point I felt that not even the greatest actor of our time could have pulled off the fake sleep gambit any longer, so I sat up in bed and asked what was the matter.

As it turned out, my initial instincts were correct. *I* was the matter. Somehow I was responsible for the myriad sadnesses in her life. I was indifferent to world hunger and political persecution. I wasn't enthusiastic enough in my support of women's rights. I made her ride the subway too often. I looked at her sister's ass at Thanksgiving. The floodgates burst open and I was drowning in my own massive culpability.

In my defense, I should point out that *if* I did look at her sister's ass at Thanksgiving, it was only to marvel at the staggering effectiveness of bulimia. I swear—that woman can't weigh more than one hundred pounds. There was never any lust in that glance. I felt sorry for her and I was mystified by her feelings of inadequacy. She's a smart, pretty lady—how come she never eats?

Anyway, as far as women's rights go, I stuffed envelopes for Hillary Freaking Clinton! I actually liked the broad! It wasn't my fault she got hosed.

And I wasn't indifferent to the problems of the world. I just didn't waste my time moaning about them. I actually tried to help whenever I could. I just never saw the point in talking about it all the time.

As for the subway thing—I have to plead guilty there. I know she hated taking the subway, but taxis are ridiculous. It's not the cost that bothers me, it's the traffic. I'd rather take my chances of catching tuberculosis on a fast-moving A train than spend an hour staring glumly through a dirty window at the same backed-up midtown street corner while sweaty cabdrivers curse in Russian.

I knew she hated the subway. And I knew she resented me every time I insisted we go down there. But if marriage is all about compromise, then why was I the only one compromising all the time? If the Guarneri String Quartet were playing at Avery Fisher Hall on Sunday at the exact same time as the Super Bowl, guess where I spent my afternoon? Exactly—Beethoven 1, Football 0. And, sure, I DVR-ed it, but it's not the same. Sports are like sweet shrimp—they're meant to be enjoyed live.

I really felt like I gave way more than my fair share in the relationship. But my wife had absolutely no interest in breaking down my emotional mathematics. The only thing she wanted to break down was me. She had come to a powerful realization while she wept onto the porcelain—and it wasn't that we were out of toilet paper. My wife wanted a divorce.

Although we *were* out of toilet paper—which also turned out to be my fault.

3

The first time I got drunk I was thirteen years old. I was at my sister's sweet sixteen party and someone left the bar unattended. I filled a brandy snifter with a mixture of rum, vodka, Jack Daniel's, Mountain Dew, and Cointreau and went to town. A videotape that my uncle recorded clearly documents the fact that I subsequently stripped naked, punched our neighbor's dog, and threw up in the swimming pool. While I have no memory of any of these events, the visual evidence is incontrovertible. I was thoroughly punished and totally embarrassed, although, to this day, I remain quite proud that I never actually passed out (and that I dropped a German shepherd with one shot).

After that trial by fire, I pretty much kept a lid on my taste for the grain and the grape. I enjoyed the occasional descent into Dionysus's lair, but nothing too extreme. A beer here, some tequila there. The only time I ever shot an eighty-two on the golf course, I celebrated by downing a half dozen shots of Jägermeister. I woke up in a sand trap with a five iron twisted around my waist like a belt. Apparently, unlike my thirteen-year-old self, the twenty-two-year-old version of me had developed the ability to pass out.

My wife was not a fan of drinking. Or, to be more specific, she was not a fan of being drunk. She loved to blather on about red wine and its nose, legs, body, bouquet, thighs, thorax, and hints of persimmon. But if you ever actually tried to drink more than one glass of the stuff, she'd glare at you like you just farted in the potato salad.

So for the eight years during which I had been married, I had been operating on a pretty steady diet of fruit juice, sparkling mineral water, and tiny sips of pinot noir hastily expectorated into pewter bowls.

Upon hearing the news that my weepy wife wanted a divorce, however, I was suddenly overcome by a massive thirst for the great taste of rum, vodka, Jack Daniel's, Mountain Dew, and Cointreau. It's just as well that I didn't have an open bar nearby because this time it might not have been the neighbor's dog who got punched.

But I kept my base urges in check. I was totally sober while my wife enumerated my infinite failings. I was clearheaded while she packed her bags and stormed out of the house. I was even-keeled when the lawyer she had already hired called me the next day to begin divorce proceedings. But on the day after that, when I found out that she had already moved in with some guy named David, I went out and got hammered.

There are lots of different kinds of hammered. There's happy hammered, wistful hammered, angry hammered, horny hammered—but the worst kind of hammered is heartbroken hammered. I achieved that sorry state at a bar in midtown Manhattan whose name is best left unmentioned due to legal restraints and general good taste.

I was walking to my office around 10:00 AM when I received the following text message: "Cming 4 jwlry 2mrw. Dnt B thr. Lvng w David. L8r 4 U." At first I thought that my cell phone had been hacked by a retard. Then I realized that the message was from my wife and, with the help of a nearby eight-year-old, I was able to break the code. For those of you whose minds haven't been jellified by modernity, allow me to translate: "Coming for jewelry tomorrow. Don't be there. Moved in with David. Later for you."

By 10:03 I was in the only open bar I could find, exhorting the barman to fill a pilsner glass with bourbon. By 10:26 I was on my third glass. By 10:34 I was shattering all three empty pilsner glasses against the wall. By 10:35 I was being punched in the face by said barman.

At around 10:50, as I was applying ice to my cheek and singing "The Gypsy Rover" with Kevin (the barman), I came to the conclusion that heartbroken hammered just wasn't working out for me. I still realized the utter necessity of getting drunk and staying drunk, but I knew that there had to be a healthier, safer, and more amusing way of going about it.

I needed to shock my heart back to where it used to be. Not where it used to be when I was being picked at and hemmed in by my wife. Not where it used to be when I was sweating over assignments or grinding out exams. I wanted— no, I *needed*—to get back that feeling I had when I was thirteen just after I punched the dog, and just before I lost my memory. I had to find a way to have some fun again. And that's when I first hatched the idea of checking out of my life for a whole year and going in search of a better one. And I decided to kick off my year of living stupidly by getting happy hammered in Ireland.

4

When I floated the idea of an alcohol-fueled Hibernian holiday around town, many of my friends wanted a piece of the action. But they're all married so one by one they each had to admit that they couldn't come along for the ride. Not one of them blamed his wife—but it was clear what was going on. They all looked like their moms had just told them they couldn't go skateboarding in the rain.

But my "mom" was shacking up with some guy named David in Williamsburg. So I could skateboard wherever the hell I wanted to. Besides, I didn't really want anyone to come along on this trip anyway.

Pretty much my entire life I have had someone tagging along with me. First it was my parents, then it was roommates in college, then it was girlfriends, then it was my wife. The only time I was ever actually alone was in the bathroom—which might explain why my wife was always complaining that I took so damn long in the bathroom.

In one fell swoop I went from never alone to way too alone. Wandering around my house wondering what she was doing and why she was doing it started eating away at my insides. I needed to get out of the rut I was in, because everything reminded me of her. Going to work, buying oranges, filling up the gas tank—it was all part of my life's routine and my life's routine was inexorably tied up with her. And trudging through it all without her made being without her hurt even more.

That's why just taking off seemed to make so much sense to me. It wasn't going to be just another two-week vacation. This was going to be the start of an entire year of vacation. Actually, it wasn't even going to be vacation. I was going to hire myself to spend a year entertaining myself. Kind of like when that English couple hired Mary Poppins to take care of their kids, only this time *I* was Mary Poppins. I was also the kids. And I guess that, technically, I was also the English couple. The point is: I decided to take a year to figure out what the hell had gone wrong with my life. I was going to break the cycle of monotony, self-recrimination, and sorrow—and the first step was to get delightfully wasted on the Emerald Isle.

I gave notice at my office. The fact that no one there really wanted to know why or bothered to try and convince me to stay further reinforced the rightness of what I was doing. It also made me feel much less guilty about stealing all those office supplies.

I bought a one-way ticket to Dublin, double-checked to make sure that my passport was still valid, packed a bag, and vowed not to return until I was convinced that my life didn't suck anymore. Then I hailed a taxi and headed to JFK. Not surprisingly, the ride took two hours in a smelly cab with an angry driver cursing in Russian the whole time. I swear—I'm not going anywhere ever again until they build a new airport much closer to Manhattan.

5

So now I'm in Ireland and Giovanna is staring at me with her great green eyes and plump Jolie lips and I'm wishing she would kiss me. I'm also wishing that I'd eaten something in the past ten hours—a piece of bread—anything. I'm definitely hammered but it's a happy hammered with a touch of wistfulness about it and maybe a tinge of heartbreak but nothing I can't handle.

This sensation of being blissfully blitzed is what my friend Colin refers to as "dancing with molasses." He equates drinking to excess with entering a time machine. Not one in which you travel to the past or the future, but a time machine that alters our perception of time and makes the present move incredibly slowly.

When you're the "right" kind of plastered, your mind and body feel like they're wrapped up in gauze—a nice, happy gauze; not a scary mummy gauze. It's almost like swimming in a pool filled with melted cheese, or getting a concussion without first having to suffer the painful blow to the head.

Reaching toward the bar to pick up your pint can take up to forty-five minutes. The flight time of a dart that you just hurled at the bull's-eye can be anywhere between one and four hours, depending on the force you applied. Shouting out a boozy hello to a beautiful girl standing underneath the "If you're lucky enough to be Irish, you're lucky enough" sign can last for days. According to Colin, if you get drunk enough in the right environment, under the right circumstances you can, in theory, live forever.

To prove Colin's point, this moment with Giovanna—the one where she's laughing and I'm laughing and her lips are about an inch away from mine and I can see that she's wearing a lavender-colored bra and that she has a freckle behind her left ear—this moment has lasted pretty much as long as I can remember. And it's showing no signs of ending. I think I'm telling her the story about the time I went fishing for stripers and accidentally caught a tiger shark instead.

I can't be sure that's the story because my brain is fuzzy and my heart is pounding and I'm thinking a million things at once about the bra and the freckle and my wife and David and the fact that alcohol is essentially liquid poison but in a good way. But it's probably the shark story because it's a very funny story and Giovanna's really laughing. See, somehow I managed to drag the fish out of the water and into the boat without realizing that, instead of an adorable striped bass, it was a vicious, multifanged tiger shark. Everybody freaked out—as well they should have—and a good time was had by all.

In real life the story had kind of a sad ending because one of the people on the charter boat had brought a teacup Yorkie along, which the shark bit in two. Then the first mate clubbed the shark to death with a Coke bottle. But when I tell the story

I usually cut out right after I land the shark so it always gets big laughs.

So I'm in that weird, bright, silly, happy, confused, thick-tongued, slightly sweaty place, and so is Giovanna. True to Colin's teachings, time suddenly stops. Or it almost stops. Everything's moving so slowly that it looks like the entire bar has been stuck in the La Brea tar pits. The neck fat on the guy with the Cork City jersey slowly ripples like a picnic blanket being shaken out in the sun. A thick drop of Beamish quivers at the edge of the tap, but never quite makes the long plummeting plop to the bar. Even the music has slowed down to an incomprehensible, deep-pitched drone. Which is a massive improvement because the song that was playing was "Saturday Night" by the Bay City Rollers. Why a shitty song from the '70s recorded by a one-hit-wonder band from Scotland was playing on a Thursday in 2008 in the middle of Ireland is anyone's guess. For the most part, Irish bars have three musical modes: synthetic dance/trance crap, horrible hits from long bygone eras, and ultratraditional Irish folk music.

That first night out drinking in Ireland, folk music is what you clamor for. Getting wrecked while ruddy guys in fishing sweaters sing about Domhnall MacLochlainn and his raid against Conaille Muirthemne is everyone's idea of the perfect evening on the Emerald Isle. But after around an hour of that shit, you're so sick of Irish folk music that you're desperate for the dance/trance crap or some played-out oldies. Surprisingly, I did not hear a single U2 song the entire time I was there.

Anyway, I'm in the bar and everything's moving as slowly as a stegosaurus caught in melted asphalt. And there's this moment where Giovanna and I both realize that this is all working out perfectly and kissing each other probably wouldn't be such a bad idea after all. We both realize this at exactly the same time—we can see it in each other's glassy eyes that are quickly losing the ability to focus. Unfortunately, we also lean in to kiss each other at exactly the same time. And that's when I accidentally head-butt her and break her nose.

6

Colin knows a great deal about Ireland. Colin knows a great deal about drinking. And Colin knows a great deal about what a middle-aged man should do in order to reconnect with his lost sense of freedom and adventure. Colin knows absolutely nothing about how to stop the flow of blood from an Italian woman's nose. His initial suggestion was to stuff a cocktail olive in each nostril.

Colin, while enjoying the Irishiest of all Irish names, is not actually Irish. That is to say, he's not from Ireland. Obviously anyone named Colin has to have some Irish in him. And isn't everyone in America at least a little bit Irish? I think that Wesley Snipes has a grandmother from Galway. But technically Colin is from Los Angeles, California. I was not aware of this fact when I met him at the Aerfort Bhaile Átha Cliath. (For those of you not in the know, Aerfort Bhaile Átha Cliath is not a breakaway former Soviet republic, nor is it an al Qaeda training center. It's just how you say Dublin International Airport in Gaeilge—or Gaelic—or whatever the hell they call their language over there. It was all explained to me many times but since I was always drunk during the explanation, and the people doing the explaining were drunk, the lesson never really sunk in.)

I was at the airport waiting for my bags when I thought I'd do some advance reconnoitering. I figured that I'd ask the most Irish-looking person I could find which Dublin pub serves the best pint. That's when I noticed Colin. To say that he looks like a leprechaun is to do him a disservice. Leprechauns have a slightly creepy, kind of hairy, dwarfish quality that I have never found appealing. In my imagination they look like a cross between Bilbo Baggins and a child molester. Colin looks more like a cross between Bilbo Baggins and Lindsay Lohan. So I guess he looks like either an extremely cute leprechaun or an extremely ugly Hollywood actress/faux lesbian.

I asked for drinking advice from this adorable wee man and I screwed up my face in concentration, prepared to sift through his impenetrable brogue in an attempt to decipher his meaning. It turned out not to be so hard to decipher.

"Dude, you gotta go to Grogan's Castle Lounge," he said with a SoCal accent that would have put Jeff Spicoli to shame.

Colin first came to visit Ireland when he was ten. His mother brought him there so that he could meet her father. Her father, who was originally from Ireland, used to live with her and her mother in New York. But one night he got drunk at his job as a switcher in the subway tunnels and forgot to re-route an A train. There was a small but unpleasant crash and he was fired. After that he faced a difficult choice: either stop drinking or lose his family. Without a moment's hesitation, he hopped on the next flight back to Ireland where he spent the next forty-five years getting blitzed. I wish I could tell you that this is all a fabrication and that I'm just co-opting a cheesy Irish stereotype, but it's true. And it gets worse: his name was Paddy.

Colin remembers that first meeting with the old Mick. His mom walked her boy into her father's favorite pub and introduced the two. Colin's grandfather looked him over from head to toe and said (in his impenetrable Irish brogue), "I thought he'd be a little more masculine."

I'd be happy to report that Colin won the old man's heart that day and they spent every summer together from then on fishing and telling tall tales full of bluster and blarney. But the truth is, the guy was a prick and he died a few months later.

But that one trip to Ireland got under Colin's skin. He went back every chance he got, each time for longer and longer stays. When I bumped into him at the airport, he had just made the official move from LA to Dublin for good. So even though he wasn't a card-carrying—or at least Irish-passport-carrying—Irishman, he was an invaluable font of first-rate Irish information.

Colin was right about Grogan's. He was right about just about everything he told me. And if he had been Irish, I'm sure that he would have told me that I was wasting my time and my money by repeatedly dialing 911 on my cell phone in an attempt to get someone to help out with Giovanna's busted nose. But, while he knew all about drinking and saving my life, there were some significant gaps in his store of knowledge.

It was the waitress who brought us some of those paper towels that everyone outside of America uses that never actually absorb anything who told me that the emergency number in Ireland is 112. As I dialed 112, however, she reminded me that in Ireland an emergency is, like, an IRA firebombing. Getting a broken nose while drinking isn't an emergency there—it's an average Thursday night. Properly chastised, I tilted Giovanna's head back, bunched up a wad of "paper" "towels" under her schnozz, and led her out into the night.

7

As predicted, we must have passed a half dozen other people with bloody and/or broken noses on our way to Mater Misericordiae Hospital.

A side note about religion in Ireland: it's very Catholic. This may sound like a foolish truism, but it's really noticeable when you're there. In America we think we're used to the omnipresence of religion, but it's really more of a ubiquitous but generalized spirituality that surrounds us. Drive through any medium-sized city and you'll see a variety of churches and temples and mosques. Keep driving and you'll probably find some yoga studios, a Buddhist retreat, and a self-help center or two. But in Ireland you find Catholic churches. And you see Catholic priests. And you see Catholic schoolkids. Everywhere. (Obviously, this is in the Republic of Ireland. I'm not sure how it breaks down up north. I know that they have their fair share of Protestants, but I bet the Buddhist/mosque quotient is still on the low side.) Pretty much everything in Ireland is named after either something old and Gaelic or something old and Catholic (a lot of times they're both).

So now I'm in the waiting area of the emergency room of Mater Misericordiae Hospital and I experience my first pang of longing for America. Because, while Mater Misericordiae Hospital has an impressive stone facade, massive arched windows, and a raking cornice, its interior reminds me of the men's room at Fenway. Strike that—Fenway smells better. And it attracts a better class of Irishmen.

The place is revolting. Giovanna is weeping and bleeding. She's still drunk, but now she's drunk, sad, hurt, confused, guilty, and slightly hysterical. As soon as the blood started to flow, I immediately went into my typical Mr. Responsible mode. After all, I was a conscientious husband for eight years. I was used to making the phone calls, and hailing the cab, and filling out the paperwork, and negotiating with the nurses for preferential treatment. I had actually gotten quite good at all the stuff that my wife expected of me. It had become second nature.

Colin had come with us to the emergency room. As I guesstimated Giovanna's height, weight, and birth date, I explained to Colin how my marital history had prepared me to deal with stuff like this. He just looked at me, perplexed. Then he pointed to Giovanna.

"But you're not married to her."

I had to acknowledge that this was an accurate statement.

Then he asked, "Are you even banging her?"

I told him that I was not. And then he said something that changed my life forever. I don't think I'm overstating the case when I say that Colin's next statement did more to free my mind from the shackles of my past than twenty years of self-actualization courses and/or tantric chanting ever could have done. He said . . .

"Then what the fuck are you doing here?"

Wow, huh? Pretty amazing. Aristotle on his most profound day never hit that kind of depth or perspicacity. And Aristotle was a full-time philosopher. I think Colin is a paralegal or something.

"Then what the fuck are you doing here?"

A crudely worded but significant question. And as soon as I heard it, I knew that the answer was obvious. I was there out of a sense of obligation. I was there because I was supposed to be there. I was there because it was "the right thing to do."

But what Colin was really asking me was, "Do you want to be here?" The answer was a resounding "No!" And, by extension, his question implied something powerful, liberating, and a little frightening. He wasn't just asking "what the fuck are you doing here?" He was also saying "you don't have to be here." And he was right. If I just left, what would happen? Nothing. Would Giovanna be angry? Maybe. But why the hell should I care? She wasn't my wife, my girlfriend, or even my friend really. I barely knew the broad! I'd spent a few boozy evenings listening to her whine about her boyfriend back home while I tried, unsuccessfully, to get into her pants. What kind of sap had I turned into that I actually escorted her to the emergency room and was sitting around worried about the quality of care she received? Hell, I didn't break her nose on purpose. If I'd been sitting and she'd been standing, she probably would have broken *my* nose.

Until Colin uttered his query, I had been doing the exact opposite of what I came to Ireland for. I was not in a bar, drinking, singing, screaming, trying to squeeze some adventure out of life. I was filling out health-insurance forms.

You know how many times I've filled out health-insurance forms? 2.4 ass-billion times—that's how many. And that's an exact number. I always took care of that stuff for my wife. I knew her social security number, her driver's license number, her insurance information—heck, I still get a Christmas card from the doctor who gave her Botox. I handled all the details and the information. I was like a human BlackBerry—except for the fact that my wife would actually touch her BlackBerry.

I was so accustomed to being the responsible one that it never occurred to me that I was no longer responsible for anyone but myself.

Had married life completely neutered me? Did all those cheese-appreciation classes and trips to the antiques markets in Rhinebeck actually alter my genetic code? Or had I always been a pussy? These are big questions, and they're difficult questions to answer—especially when you're sponging blood out of your brown suede wingtips while hemorrhaging drunks shriek in Gaelic. I knew one thing, though. I was going to find out the answers.

I turned to Colin and gave him my reply.

"I'll tell you what the fuck I'm doing here. I'm getting the fuck out of here! Come on!"

And, with that, I tossed Giovanna's medical forms onto the lap of an unconscious nonagenarian who looked like he could have played John Wayne's grandfather in *The Quiet Man* and led Colin out of the most foul-smelling emergency room this side of Doodyville.

8

Okay, so two minutes after I left the hospital, I raced back in there and sat by Giovanna's bedside until one of her roommates showed up to take care of her. What do you want from me? Thirty-plus years of being a good boy don't die easy. But just coming to the realization that I didn't *have* to be responsible for someone else all the time anymore had a sobering effect on me. And, by sobering effect, obviously I mean the opposite.

Q: What do you do after you have willfully acted like a callous heel for the first time in your life only to discover that, instead of being wracked by guilt, you feel fantastic? A: You take your recreational drinking to a whole new level.

This is not advice that I would offer to high school or college students. I don't feel like seminarians or active-duty soldiers currently billeted in war zones would benefit from this suggestion. But, for middle-aged chumps like me who have suddenly realized that they've spent most of their lives acting like saps, suckers, and/or patsies, this is an ideal solution.

the weeks and months following my abandonment of
anna to the hands (both literal and figurative) of the Irish
National Health Service, I hit the pubs hard. From Davy
Byrne's to the Stag's Head, from Walshes to Oliver St. John
Gogarty, I made a conscious effort to maintain a steady level
of inebriation throughout my waking hours. And I didn't sleep
much.

I fell into a routine that allowed me to perform at maximum capacity. It was probably similar to the routines that
world-class athletes develop when they're training intensively
for the Olympics. The only difference is, instead of stretching, eating right, and working out, I would drink thirty-two
different kinds of beer and whiskey all day and night, with the
occasional dose of fish and chips thrown in (for protein).

My average day would begin around noon. The fact that I
could actually sleep until noon was somewhat miraculous given
that Dublin is extremely loud and none of its windows actually shut all the way. Without a doubt, Las Vegas is the
window-seal capital of the world. Dublin is the getting-drunk-
at-breakfast capital of the world. Hey, we all have our areas of
expertise.

I would then attempt to clean my body to whatever degree
was possible. This degree was never particularly high. During
my time in Ireland, I stayed in a quaint attic apartment in
Temple Bar. It had beautiful views across the Liffey, and James
Joyce had once stayed there. Of course, if you trust the bro-
chures, James Joyce once stayed at every single place in Dublin.
Rumor has it that he wrote *Ulysses* at the Burger King on
O'Connell Street. My charming apartment had a great deal of
charming charm. What it didn't have was a serviceable bathroom. There was a tiny tub that Verne Troyer could barely fit
in, with a showerhead so low that the aforementioned Verne

Troyer would have had to kneel to wash his hair (if he had any). In order to make this analogy resonate, it's important to know that Verne Troyer is the actor who played Mini Me in the Austin Powers movies. He is very small. The fact that the dimensions of the tub were ridiculous was kind of besides the point as there was rarely any hot water.

But I'd splash some water on or around my body and I'd head to the pub. I worked out a strategy that allowed me to take in at least six pubs a day. At that rate I figured I could visit every pub in Dublin by the year 3017.

Usually I met up with Colin somewhere along the way. We wouldn't call each other. I barely even used my cell phone the entire time I was in Ireland—which is a shame because the country's cell coverage is stupendous. But somehow Colin would just find me. And wherever he went, good times followed.

There's an old Irish word that the old Irish throw around all the time over there. It's *craic*. Pronounced like "crack," craic is one of those words that doesn't have an exact definition but everyone always wants to translate for you. Basically it means "fun." But not fun like the fun you'd have throwing a Nerf football to your nephew. Craic is the kind of fun you have at two in the morning when you're so toasted you can barely stand up and someone suggests that you all go outside for a knife-throwing contest and every single one of you thinks this is an *awesome* idea. That's the kind of fun they mean when they say craic.

And I have to tell you—they're on to something. Sure, knife throwing sounds like an idiotic idea when you're on your way to the office in your three-piece suit with your rolled-up newspaper and your thermos full of decaf. But if you're in the right mood, with the right group of people, and the right kind of fuel pumping through your veins, it can be a blast. I actually embedded a steak knife about half an inch into Colin's left forearm, and he was laughing harder than I was! That's craic, man. The craic would last until they closed down whatever pub we were in. This usually happened earlier than I expected. A lot of places shut it down by midnight. The latest anywhere would be open was 2:30 in the morning. But there's one thing you have to remember about Ireland—it's full of Irish people. And they don't take the closing of every single bar in their country as a sign that they should stop drinking. Oh, no. That's what the streets, and the parks, and the garages, and the phone booths, and the riverbank, and the bridges, and the steps in front of the police station are for. So the cracking good craictimes would continue al fresco until all the alcohol was gone. Then I would stumble back to my James Joyce Autograph Charming Apartment, and I would fall blissfully asleep until the sun, the chirping birds, and the urban cacophony would wake me once again at the craic of noon.

9

Let me leave the description of my good times for a moment to address a pressing concern. I fear that I have been inhospitable in my portrayal of my wife (ex-wife). I don't want to sound like one of those guys who complains about what an evil, crazy bitch he turned out to be married to. I hear that all the time and I can't help but wonder, "If she was so horrible, why did you marry her?" They make it seem like, just because it ended badly, there was never anything good there. And that was definitely not the case with my marriage.

So, for the record, my ex-wife is not an evil, crazy bitch. When we first met, I thought that she was smart, beautiful, sensitive, creative, and interesting. And I was right. I'm still right. She still is a smart, beautiful, sensitive, creative, and interesting person. I just never noticed that she's also the single most self-obsessed person on planet earth. And I'm factoring Sharon Stone and Kim Jong Il into this equation.

All things considered, my wife and I had a pretty good run. Out of the eight years together, I'd say that two were just flat-out fantastic. One was forgettable—as in absolutely nothing happened and I have forgotten the whole thing. Three were dry, cruel, spiteful, loveless, and bitter. And then things got bad.

You know how supposedly a bear will gnaw through its own leg to free itself from a trap? Well, in retrospect, I probably should have given that a shot. Because I can always buy a pros-thetic leg, but I'm never getting those 730 days back.

As a man, my default position is "I'm always right." But as a married man I made a conscious choice to reset my de-fault position to "my wife is always right." So right off the bat I created a certain amount of inevitable conflict in the relationship.

But was that really my fault? If she had tweaked her default position from "my needs come first" to "his needs come first," then we might have made a go of it. But, as we all know, only pimply geeks with graduate degrees from Stanford should play around with your default settings. If you try and do it, it'll just screw up your hard drive and you'll delete some key files.

Okay, this computer analogy is getting exhausted—but I'm not quite done with it yet. I thought about this a lot during my year of drinking, playing, etc. And I came to the conclu-sion that, ultimately, men are not from Mars and women are not from Venus. It's more like, some people are Macs and some people are PCs. These differences aren't based on sex. It's to-tally random.

Due to advances in technology (and human development), the Macs and PCs are not wholly incompatible. It just takes some work to get the two operating systems to communicate with each other. And sometimes even the best intentions aren't enough to overcome software glitches.

Jesus, I'm really deep in it now, aren't I? Let me explain a little more in a desperate attempt to make this make sense. I'm a Mac guy. And sometimes I have had to work on a Microsoft Word document with PC people. Now, super-smart trillion-aires have toiled long and hard to make Microsoft Word function on both platforms. So going back and forth was a breeze. But every now and then, for absolutely no reason, bizarre things would happen. Like, I would rewrite a paragraph and, when I sent it to the PC people, they would open their screen and see a thousand letter *p*'s arranged to look like the profile of Abraham Lincoln. (This happened only once, but it did happen.)

We could always restore the file, and usually we didn't have any more problems, but there's a basic difference there that can't be ignored. Sometimes Macs and PCs simply can't get on the same page. Sometimes people just aren't meant to share their lives together. Especially if the PCs insist on sleeping with some guy named David.

Anyway, the whole computer analogy is a long way of saying, I don't hate my ex-wife. I did at the start of my journey. And some of that animosity still flares back up every now and then out of the blue—usually when I meet someone named David. But, for the most part, I have learned to accept that we were just two people operating in different electronic planes.

All of which is a roundabout way of getting to Alicia.

10

Meeting Alicia, like everything that happened to me in Ireland, was the result of drinking. After three months, I started feeling that Dublin was a little claustrophobic. I was known by my first name in almost every pub I visited. And there were at least a dozen spots where they had already crafted a nickname for me. This nickname was different at each locale, except for two bars where both groups of creative geniuses in charge of naming rights came up with "The Yank." My favorite of all these nicknames was "The Goat," which everyone at McDaid's called me. I have no recollection of why they called me the Goat, but they were so committed to it that someone had it stenciled onto a beer glass which they gave me on what they whimsically and erroneously decided was my birthday.

I was snug and content with my Dublin routine, but I was starting to feel a little hemmed in. Knowing that Ireland is famous for its gorgeous countryside as well as its gorgeous alcohol, I decided to take a road trip through the great green greenery.

Once again, Colin's assistance proved to be invaluable.

"Why the hell would you want to drive around the countryside? What are you—an idiot?"

When I explained my situation, he was much more accommodating.

"Jesus, you still sound like a moron," he said. "If you really need to go for a trip, why don't you at least take a tour of the Whiskey Trail?"

Now, *that's* what I love about Ireland. They've found a way to incorporate drinking into every single possible activity that a man or woman could even dream of participating in. In America, trail hiking is the sole purview of granola-munching, bottled water–swilling health nuts. In Ireland, even the drunks look forward to it.

And speaking of drunks, whiskey, and Ireland, they get extremely worked up over the spelling of that specific intoxicated distilled spirit. The Irish (and most Americans) spell it with an *e* instead of just "whisky." If, for reasons that I can't imagine, you were to write down the word "whisky" in Ireland, and you were to leave out the *e,* they would all laugh at you. I suppose that if you were mute, and wanted to get your Jameson on, you might need to write it down. Or perhaps if you were working at a pub and taking a big order I guess you might write it down . . . Just remember—the Irish use an *e.*

The Scottish, however, do not. They invented the stuff, and they're adamant about spelling it "whisky." Since the Scots are, like, the OGs of "whisky," I guess we should all defer to them. But it feels like the Irish drink more of the stuff than everyone else combined, so, as far as I'm concerned, whiskey it is, and whiskey it shall remain.

As for the Whiskey Trail, what can I tell you? All you need to know about this marvelous adventure is that there is actually a place called Bushmills Village. That's right—there's an adorable, eponymous seaside town where they've been making that sweet elixir for around six hundred years.

Can you imagine if there was a town in America called Dorito Corners? Or Twinkieburg? There would be a line of tourists in pickup trucks and RVs stretching to the next county. Pilgrims would come from all corners of the earth to taste the freshest chips and "pastries" at their very birthplace. Obviously Doritoville and Twinkieburg couldn't exist because Doritos and Twinkies haven't been made in the same process with the same painstaking eye for detail for centuries the way Bushmills has. Doritos and Twinkies are made out of chemicals in big machines in factories in the middle of nowhere. Not a lot of tourist trail possibilities there.

But whiskey . . . that stuff is created in some of the most spectacular spots you'll ever see. The buildings are stunning. The scenery is breathtaking. And the alcohol is cheap and plentiful. It's also delicious—at least that's what the experts say. I've always viewed this as an extremely subjective matter.

I love being drunk. I love getting drunk. I love hanging out with drunks. I don't always love the taste of alcohol. Give me a comfy pub, a thick steak, a roaring fire, some dudes playing darts for money, and a chipped glass full of whiskey and I'm a happy man. Give me six splashes of whiskey in six different snifters, a snooty whiskey sommelier, and a fancy postmodern whiskey tasting room and I'm gonna wish I was back by the roaring fire. Because, as far as I'm concerned, whiskey just doesn't taste that great. It's the whole whiskey zeitgeist that I enjoy.

By and large, they keep things pretty homey on the Whiskey Trail. And they certainly keep the whiskey flowing. I started up north and slowly worked my way southward. After a week or two, I was somehow still conscious by the time we rolled into Midleton, just east of Cork. I don't remember exactly who was doing the driving, but I'm pretty sure that he (or she) remained sober. Also, I seem to recall that we traversed the lush, wet countryside on some kind of smallish tour bus. I tried to sleep as much as possible during the drive to marshal my forces for maximum drinkability.

The Old Midleton Distillery used to be the primary plant for Jameson. That means that it's ground zero for Irish whiskey. Which means that, for every cop, fireman, clog dancer, tenor, Massachusetts senator, and white bantamweight boxer, this place is like Eden, Jerusalem, the confluence of the Tigris and the Euphrates, and Mount Ararat all rolled into one. There's a spiritual, almost reverential, quality to the buildings and grounds. It feels as much like a holy site as anywhere I've ever been in my life. Plus they've got one hell of a gift shop.

I was in the gift shop purchasing a Jameson-branded silver hip flask, which they swore was just like the one that James Joyce, George Bernard Shaw, W. B. Yeats, and the guy from the Irish Spring commercials used to use, when I met Alicia.

A quick word about me and the ladies: there is no me and the ladies. I was completely faithful during the eight years of my marriage (and during the three and a half years that we dated before getting married). I'm not bragging or anything. This is just the way I'm built. The thought of being with other women truly never occurred to me on any practical level. I had my girl, and that was that.

After I discovered that "my girl" was banging some guy named David, naturally I went through the delightful roundelay of emotions that follow: anger, sadness, confusion, a sense of worthlessness, and a desire for revenge. The revenge angle was going to be sweet and it was comprised primarily of me having sex with most of my wife's friends and definitely her sister. However, the way I'm built is the way I'm built. The whole concept of revenge sex seemed like a good idea in the hypothetical. But when the time came to put plans into action, I immediately realized that none of it was ever going to happen.

If you're walking down Tenth Avenue and you look at some guys a certain way, they'll punch you in the face. If you look at other guys the same way, they'll just walk on by. I'm a walk-on-by guy. I'm not built to punch you in the face for no reason. Sure, I'll toss a knife at my friends, under the proper supervision, and only if I've got a few drinks in me. But I'm not built to do back flips off of the top deck of a booze cruise in Cabo. I'm not built to have meaningless sex with a bunch of women I barely know just to get back at my wife. Sometimes I wish I was built like that, but I'm not and I know it and that's that. Perhaps those other guys are jealous of the fact that I'm pretty good at Scrabble.

The truth of the matter is that the spot in my heart reserved for love and romance and sex had, for over a decade, been filled by one woman. And just because she was now getting filled by someone else, it wasn't any easier to renovate that space for new tenants.

So ever since my wife asked for a divorce, I had been celibate. Technically speaking, I had been celibate for at least three months before that. Like I said—those last couple of years were not pretty. I probably would have had to back up the final nookie date at least six more months if it hadn't been for a certain rowdy evening in mid-March. We were at a Caribbean-themed office party and the missus got a little tipsy on two portions of some extremely strong rum cake. One thing led to another and my yearly marital sex quota was filled.

My infatuation with Giovanna was entirely alcohol induced. As drunk as I was most of the time, I still realized that nothing was going to happen between us. The main reason for this was how incredibly tedious she was to be around if one (or, God forbid, *both*) of us was sober. I know that there are a lot of different kinds of pasta in Italy. That doesn't mean you have to talk about them all the time, does it? Yeah, great, whatever—they make pasta shaped like ears and hats. Big whoop. You ever hear of an invading army storming a castle to get its hands on a vast store of hidden pappardelle? I thought not. But the Irish have been killing one another for centuries over whiskey. And that brings us back to Midleton and Alicia.

I I

I was in the gift shop browsing through a spinning carousel rack that housed a surprisingly extensive collection of books about alcohol, about to pay for my flask, when I heard someone with a broad Midwestern accent ask, "Excuse me, sir. Would you mind moving out of the way?"

I looked up and saw a beautiful young woman with long black hair and stunning hazel eyes. I smiled involuntarily and said something suave and sophisticated like, "Huh?"

"Can you move, please? You're right in the middle of our shot."

Maybe it was the long layoff from getting laid, or maybe it was all the drinks I'd been drinking, but I completely didn't understand what she was talking about. I heard "shot" and assumed she was referring to a shot of whiskey. But how could I be in the middle of her shot of whiskey? I actually looked around me as if I expected to find small glasses filled with amber

liquid hovering in the air. Then she took pity on me and spoke
to me as if I were a small child, or a drunk grown-up.

"We're filming a documentary here. And you're kind of in
the way of the shot we're trying to get. Sorry."

That's when I noticed that a film crew was standing right
next to the lovely woman with the hazel eyes. I don't know
how I missed them—there was a cameraman, a guy adjusting
some lights, and another guy holding a long fuzzy boom.

"Of course," I replied. "*I'm* sorry." I remember thinking
that this was an extremely gentlemanly thing to say. I then
gracefully slid out of the way. Unfortunately, as I slid away
gracefully, I also smashed into the spinning carousel rack,
knocking it and myself to the floor and sending the flask and
every single book about alcohol flying across the gift shop.

The lady helped me to my feet and asked if I was okay. I
immediately noticed that she smelled like orange blossoms,
which, along with night-blooming jasmine and fresh-cut grass,
is one of the three all-time great smells ever created. I also
noticed that I was grinning like an orangutan on thorazine.

"Why don't you sit down? It looks like you've been hitting
the Whiskey Trail pretty hard." She smiled as she said this—
but, for some reason, when she smiled she didn't look like a
sedated primate. She just looked pretty and nice. I can't recall
with total accuracy, but after the disarming smile I think that
I actually rested my head against her shoulder and breathed in
deeply. The fact that she didn't mace me instantly is a real
testament to her forgiving nature.

"Easy, big boy. Barry, want to give me a hand here?" She
called to her cameraman who helped ease me over to a bench
next to some old maps and an array of playing cards featuring
the images of great Irish writers who were also drunks. (Those

guys are like superstars in Ireland, which shows you what an addiction-tolerant society it is. Brendan Behan once famously described himself as "a drinker with writing problems," and they teach him in schools. Britney Spears has one beer and we want to take her kids away.)

"Are you okay?" the sweet-smelling documentarian asked. I nodded foolishly. Frankly, I'm surprised I didn't stomp my foot once for yes, like a trained circus pony. Seriously, this woman had me acting like a seventh grader with serious self-esteem issues. I decided that the time had come to rally the troops and get my act together. I introduced myself and thanked her for her help. She introduced herself and apologized for asking me to move to begin with.

"There's nothing more annoying than a film crew that thinks it's more important than everyone else. You give some people a walkie-talkie and they act like they rule the world. Can you imagine how much more damage Hitler could have done if he'd had a script supervisor and an assistant director?"

Now, I'll acknowledge that this is not the kind of thing that most people say to other people whom they have just met at whiskey distilleries in County Cork. Usually, off-color comments like these are reserved for private moments with close friends. And I can see why some might bridle at the suggestion that Hitler would have been even more evil if he had employed an IATSE crew. I, however, laughed out loud. I may have even snorted.

"I'm sorry," Alicia said. "That was totally inappropriate. I'm exhausted and the whiskey fumes must be getting to me. I think I need some fresh air."

Like a kitten eyeing a ball of string or Brendan Behan eyeing a goatskin filled with Inishowen, I pounced.

"Why don't we go outside for a walk?"

Once again she did not mace me, which was extremely kind of her. Instead we went outside and walked along the banks of the Dungourney River for the next hour. We talked about all kinds of things, although the primary topic of conversation was why we were both in the Old Midleton Distillery at two in the afternoon on a Wednesday.

She told me all about the documentary that she was making in which she was highlighting great, underexposed travel destinations. I told her all about how my wife was sleeping with some guy named David. (Although by this point, I think that my wife had already screwed over David as well and was on some kind of whirlwind transcontinental spiritual journey. Yet one more idea of mine that she copied that I'll never get any credit for.)

A few observations gleaned from my afternoon with Alicia.

1) That hour I spent walking and talking with her was probably the first waking hour I spent in Ireland when I did not drink anything, want to drink anything, or even think about drinking anything.

2) She made me feel stupid—but in a good way. Giovanna made me feel stupid in a bad way because when I was around her I was always drunk, and acting like a moron, and not being myself. Alicia made me feel stupid because she was clearly smarter and more clever than I am, which made me want to get smarter and more clever.

3) Alicia had an uncanny ability to make me appreciate my surroundings. Before I met her, I was just excited to be in the place where they made the whiskey. After I met her, I actually noticed the beauty of the place where they made the whiskey.

4) Damn, she smelled good.

After a while it became clear that, regardless of Colin's theory of the relativity of time as it pertains to alcohol, the clocks had not stopped when I met Alicia. She had to get back to work. They were just beginning the segment of their film about Ireland's Whiskey Trail. They had started in Cork and were filming several nearby distilleries. I had just finished my sojourn down the Whiskey Trail. She had to interview a vice president of Jameson, and I had to get back to Dublin to take care of some last-minute travel arrangements for the next leg of my yearlong trip to nowhere.

The timing could not have been worse. Not that there was anything for the timing to screw up. It's not like our eyes met amidst the froth and foam of the Dungourney River and we pledged our eternal devotion to each other. Nor did we rip each other's clothes off and make sweet, mad love on the banks of said Dungourney. The Dungourney's not really much of a river, anyway. It doesn't provide a very convincing backdrop for grand romantic gestures and/or passionate boffing. And, like I said, we just talked.

But I would have liked to talk to her more. I would have liked to hear about the other great, underexposed travel destinations upon which she would be shining her cinematic light. I would have liked to grin like a moron while she explained the differences between high definition video formats, while I surreptitiously sniffed her delicate scent of citrus flowers. But that's not the way it happened. I went off to Dublin, and she went off to Ballymacoda, or Ballynaparka, or Ballykilmurry (I know that it was one of the Ballys but there are a lot of them in Ireland and it's hard to keep track).

12

When I returned to Dublin, I couldn't help but notice a different vibe in the air. It was kind of like that last week at summer camp when everyone's still playing softball and swimming in the lake, but you can tell they're all thinking about going back to school. The difference in this case is that no one in Dublin plays softball. Also, instead of heading to school, I was about to go to Las Vegas.

I wasn't going to get hung up on the details of my trip, though. My whole life until that point had been all about the details. I had calendars at work and schedules at home. My wife and my secretary knew where I was every second of every day. And if, God forbid, someone couldn't locate me by cell phone, e-mail, or GPS device, I would hear about it. Surprisingly, as controlling as my wife could be, my secretary was much more annoying when it came to keeping tabs on me.

So I was perfectly happy to have my upcoming travel plans almost totally unorganized. The only plans I had made involved my housing in Vegas. I figured that if I was going to go to the mecca of gambling, playtime, and wager-based recreation, I owed it to myself to stay in the holiest of holy hotels. I called in a favor from an old client in Vegas and asked him if he could hook me up at the Bellagio Hotel. He had recently left a message saying the room would be available soon. So it was time to move on.

Just before I left Dublin, I experienced one of my most pleasant evenings of wild-eyed inebriation. I had received a message from Colin to meet him at Grogan's. It wasn't a text message, or a voice- or e-mail. It was the usual kind of message I got while living in Ireland. I bumped into my landlady, a wonderful older woman with the staggeringly unlikely name of Teagan Scorcese (no relation to Martin). After conversing for what felt like seven hours about the possibility that it might or might not but it definitely might rain, I finally managed to break away by telling her that I had to take my emphysema medication. Of course, I don't have emphysema—but Teagan does and she clearly had forgotten to take her medication. I figured that, by broaching the subject, it might trigger her memory and she'd live to bake shepherd's pie another day. My strategy worked. As she headed back to her apartment she suddenly remembered something else. "Oh, that little, wee Colin feller stopped by for ya. Ay, he's a delight that one— though I canna unnerstan' him so well sometime. He wants for you to meet him up to Grogan's." And that's how I got my messages. It was a lot more time consuming than checking my e-mail, but far more entertaining.

I headed out to meet Colin around nine PM. The sky was just starting to darken and the streets were full of people. As I walked down Anglesea Street, I passed a new bar that had just opened up. They were having some kind of private, invitation-only party and I watched the action for a few minutes through the floor-to-ceiling plate-glass windows in front. It was an extremely sophisticated, minimalist, modern space. Lots of polished steel, white plaster, and blond wood. And it appeared to be a wine bar. Dozens of slender, attractive people were swirling whites and reds in elegant goblets. A great deal of serious conversing seemed to be taking place. The front door was open, but I couldn't hear any sounds emerging from within. From the look of the patrons, I could imagine that the new ballet season and the relative merits of acidophilus were being discussed while Scandinavian jazz played softly through the speakers.

The whole thing looked like a hundred parties that my wife and I attended back in New York—except there weren't as many beautiful gay people or charismatic Puerto Ricans. I kept watching for a while until I was distracted by the sounds of someone hollering, "Hey! Get your ass in here already!" It was Colin, delivering a new message the old-fashioned way. He was leaning out of the front door of Gogarty's and shouting down Anglesea to get my attention. Behind him I could see that the place was packed. The sounds of laughter, cursing, and music poured out from the pub. I could smell the fireplace, and the carving station, and the strangely appealing scent of beer-soaked floors.

"Come on already. I've been buying pints for an hour and I need you to take over. Also, there's eight dudes from Australia in here and I promised you'd tell them about the time you punched a dog!"

I moved away from the wine bar and headed off to join Colin who already had two glasses of Guinness waiting for me. As it turned out, they were both for him. But I more than made up for my late start. And the Australians enjoyed the dog story.

We sat by the fireplace and drank, and sang, and bullshitted until they booted us out of there at 2:30 in the morning. Then about twenty of us kept the party going for a few more hours by the banks of the Liffey. We sang more preposterous Irish folk songs and bet on who could skip rocks more times across the river's surface. Two policemen came by to shut us up, but I snuck them a bottle of Midleton Rare and took five euros off of one of them when my eight-skipper just edged out his seven. We broke it up as the sun rose, all promising to be best friends forever—even if we never saw one another again. Which we didn't.

As I prepared to move out of my attic apartment in Temple Bar, I realized how much I was going to miss Ireland. There's a pace of life there that's quite unlike anywhere else I've ever been. Much like the Swiss, the French, and the Spanish, the Irish put a real emphasis on appreciating and enjoying their lives. But while the Swiss bank, and the French make overrated movies, and the Spaniards sleep their preposterous siestas, the Irish drink. It's the cornerstone of their national identity. The Irish drink the way Americans work and invade sovereign nations. It's what they're all about.

After almost four months of joining them in their national obsession, I came to a significant realization: you don't have to be Irish, or even in Ireland, to drink like the Irish. The best part of the whole thing isn't even the drinking—it's the camaraderie and the open, accepting attitude toward friends and fun. But I also realized that it was time to move on. My heart felt freer than it had in years. That was kind of the point of all that hanging out and drinking and telling crazy stories and singing weird songs. They've figured out over there how to free your soul regardless of the nefarious forces that are always lurking, trying to enslave it again. So my heart felt free. Unfortunately, the rest of my body felt like it had been beaten by marauding Vikings. My extended drinking binge was like that movie *Supersize Me,* only instead of going to McDonald's, I went to McEwan's (this joke works best if you know that McEwan's is a kind of beer). I had gained fifteen pounds. My skin was pale and clammy. I was getting the night sweats on a regular basis and my hair had started thinning. In short, I was starting to turn Irish. So it was time to go.

I took my leave from Colin at the same place where I first saw him—the world's most poorly named airport, the Aerfort Bhaile Átha Cliath. He had convinced me to have a "good-bye nip" at the Jameson Bar. He got me so ripped that I almost missed my flight. As I staggered through the security checkpoint, Colin bid me farewell with a typical Irish saying: "May the Lord keep you in His hand, and never close His fist too tight."

He smiled and waved. Then for a second it looked like he was going to throw up on a young Asian woman's duffel bag, but he righted the ship and turned back to me. As I rushed off to my boarding gate, I could hear him yell, "You'll be okay, Bobby! Just don't forget to enjoy your *craic!*"

That Colin is a sweet, sweet man. I just wish that craic didn't sound exactly like "crack" because before they let me on the plane, airport security strip-searched me and performed an extensive cavity probe.

Book Two

Las Vegas

or

"I can't believe that God plays dice
with the universe."
— Albert Einstein

or

12 Tales About Chasing the Dragon

13

It's always nice to discover that those weird personality quirks you attempt to keep hidden because you always feared that they were sure signs of rapidly advancing schizophrenic delusion are actually shared by others. For example, you can't imagine my relief when I came across this quotation from Fyodor Dostoyevsky:

> Even as I approach the gambling hall, as soon as I hear, two rooms away, the jingle of money poured out on the table, I almost go into convulsions.

Me too, FyDo! I get the exact same jittery, sweaty, heart-pounding feeling like I want to run as fast as I can but I'm also about to black out when I'm still approaching the first of the six different sets of glass doors that lead to every Vegas casino. All I hear is the faintest hint of the cacophony generated within by slot machine payouts and shrieking hillbillies who just hit the hard eight and I start to get dizzy, anxious, and excited.

When I was little, all I cared about was playing basketball. After school I'd race out to the local YMCA to find a pickup game. And I'd get that same nervous, desperate feeling as I approached the gym and heard the first sounds of squeaking sneakers. Later, when I started fixating on golf, it was the smell of fresh-cut grass and the *thwack* of iron against Titleist that drove me bananas. But ever since my first visit to a real live, big boy casino, the distinctive melodic melange of money, kitsch, and heartbreak has trumped all other saliva-inducing sensations. It's a comforting feeling to know that I suffer from the same crippling neurosis as one of the great Russian whack-jobs/geniuses of the nineteenth century.

As soon as I came up with the idea of taking a year off to try and inject some fun into my life, I knew that Vegas had to be the centerpiece of my journey. It's not like I was some kind of Vegas junkie. I'd been there only a handful of times in my entire life—and never for more than a day or two. I had friends in Los Angeles who practically commuted. They used to brag about how they'd drive to Burbank airport, toss their car keys to the valet, hop on the next Southwest flight, and be gambling in an hour. Given the tremendous distances and the horrible traffic in LA, it actually took some of these guys less time to get to Vegas than it took them to drive to work every morning. Of course, at work they actually accumulated money.

But I'd always been too responsible and mature to burn my hard-earned cash away. I was saving for my family's future. I had a wife to support. I assumed that children were around the corner as well. Not only did I hardly ever go to Vegas, but I literally never went to Atlantic City. Not once—and that's only a two-and-a-half-hour drive from Manhattan (two hours if you're really desperate and have E-ZPass). Aside from the fact that I had always heard it was kind of gross, I just wasn't "that kind of guy." You know—the kind of guy who would call in sick, barrel down to A. City, and blow five grand at craps. I didn't even know how to play craps.

But that was all going to change now. I was going to log some hard-core casino hours. Also, I was going to learn how to play craps. There were always several gaps in my knowledge that I feared meant I was less than a real man. First among these informational sinkholes was: I didn't know how to play craps. I knew that it looked very cool and it involved the throwing of dice and the shouting of bizarre, incomprehensible sayings that everyone seemed to comprehend but me. I had kind of tried to figure it out once or twice when I was in Vegas, but the action went by way too fast. One time I asked for an explanation from a grizzled old man wearing a captain's hat and a soiled Member's Only jacket that advertised, "Tucson's Only All-Nude Cabaret." He completely ignored me up until the point where he rolled the dice. I don't know what numbers came up, but they couldn't have been good. Because Creepy Grampa started cursing me out like the sailor that he inevitably had been. He also called me a "mush," a pronouncement with which everyone else seemed to agree. I left the table more perplexed than ever.

My second embarrassing failure was: I couldn't drive a stick shift. It's not like I had tried for years and was unable to figure it out. I just never learned how. It seemed like all the "real" drivers were sophisticated Europeans doing something mysterious with their right hands and left feet, while I was stuck plodding along like a tacky American behind the wheel of a minivan. (Obviously this is a metaphor—I have never driven, nor will I ever drive, a minivan. I've always been partial to

Volvos and I will not apologize for this to anyone. They're damn fine cars and they have plenty of pep. I just always drove Volvos with automatic transmissions.)

So even though I have loved casinos from the start, I hardly ever visited them. But I was going to visit them all, I thought to myself as I winged my way through the night sky. I couldn't find a direct flight from Dublin to Vegas so I purposely booked a connection through Atlanta. That way I wouldn't be tempted to break up my trip for a quick sightseeing expedition. No offense to Atlanta, but I have never been there nor do I ever want to go there. For me, Atlanta is, like, the minivan of cities. I think I developed my anti-Atlanta bias as a youngster watching the Atlanta Hawks play in front of fifty people at the Omni. What the hell were all those Atlantans so busy doing that they couldn't take a ten-minute drive to root on Dominique Wilkins and Spud Webb? Lazy Georgian bastards. Also, the whole "tomahawk chop" thing really annoys me.

Here's one thing that doesn't annoy me: they have gambling at McCarran Airport. You can sing the praises of other airports all you want. Sure, the Reykjavík Airport is so clean you could eat off the floor. And given the quality of Icelandic food, eating off the floor might be an improvement. And, yes, I'm aware that Paris's Charles de Gaulle has an awesome Sheraton Hotel in the middle of it that's shaped like a boat and has ultra-soundproof windows. But, people—at McCarran Airport THEY HAVE GAMBLING! I don't care that it's just slot machines and video poker—they have more than thirteen hundred machines. At most airports the most you can hope to achieve is to find a flexible book light at the Brookstone. At McCarran you could win a million dollars.

Here's my first experience as an unfettered male hell-bent on gambling in Las Vegas: I spent an hour and twenty minutes playing the Wheel of Fortune slots and I ended up losing $300. At one point I was up to $580. My brain told me to quit. But my heart told my brain that $280 profit was meaningless and we should keep going. My brain was pretty adamant about cashing out. But my heart convinced it that we'd all be happier quitting when we hit $1,000. By the time we dipped below $40, my brain had my heart in a full nelson and was applying vigorous blows to its head and neck. By the time the last credit disappeared into the dark machine's gaping maw, none of my internal organs were speaking to one another. I looked around me and, for the first time, noticed that quite a lot of time had passed. I was so tantalized and distracted by the slots that I almost forgot to retrieve my luggage.

When I got to the carousel the area was empty. Fortunately, my bags were still making their lonely journey around the conveyer belt. As I loaded them onto my cart, I heard someone say: "First time in Vegas, huh?"

And that's how I met Rick. For some reason, I tend to meet important people in my life in the baggage-claim area of major international airports. To my knowledge, most people usually meet only family members, limo drivers, or cheap hookers at baggage claim. Me—that's where I met my guru.

14

Like I said before, I am not very comfortable with using the word "guru." Frankly, it's the kind of word that my wife would use. A lot. Without any sense of irony, or self-deprecation, or recognition of the preposterousness and pomposity of a middle-class New Yorker announcing that they suddenly have a guru. And yet, the word works. What's a better word for someone who changes your life and helps make the bad things good? Friend? Father? Lover? Rick isn't just another friend. I have a bunch of friends, and none of them could have shown me the way to what I was searching for like Rick did. I already had a father figure (he happened to be my father) and Rick was noth-ing like him. For starters, he didn't wear sweater vests all the time or drink three martinis at lunch while insisting, "That's the way business was conducted in my day—drinks, cigarettes, and a firm handshake between white men!" And, while I can honestly say that Rick and I have love for each other, it's a purely platonic love. We're just a couple of decent straight guys trying to have some fun and make it through the day—despite the fact that, for a second over by the McCarran baggage carousel, I thought Rick might be a gay hooker trying to pick me up.

I mean, let's face it—when a good-looking, well-muscled young man in flip-flops, a sleeveless T-shirt, and cargo shorts asks you, "First time in Vegas, huh?" in a deserted airport baggage-claim area, what are you supposed to think? He clearly wasn't working for the mayor's office welcoming new arrivals. My first reaction was that I thought maybe I had accidentally used some kind of secret Larry Craig gay airport code. Like, everybody knows that if you wait until the place is empty to pick up your bags from carousel three, it means you're looking to party. And maybe if you use a luggage cart it means you want to "receive." What the hell do I know? Just because I spent most of my life as a New York liberal doesn't mean I can't experience the occasional bout of homosexual panic.

But Rick was way ahead of me (a situation that I would rapidly grow accustomed to). "Take it easy, bro. I'm not a gay hooker. I'm just waiting for my golf clubs."

I will always give a fellow golfer the benefit of the doubt, so I explained to Rick that I had been in Vegas a couple of times before. I asked him why he thought I was a first-timer.

"Well, you have the look of a man who just spent a few hours playing the slots at the airport. And the only people who play the slots at the airport are airport employees—who wouldn't be retrieving luggage. Or first-timers."

The man is like Sherlock Holmes, if Sherlock Holmes had picked the winning Super Bowl team seven years in a row and spent his junior year of college living out of the back of a Chevy Impala.

I told him that he was basically on the money. While I had been to Vegas before, it was only a few times and for brief stays. And I admitted that I had been bewitched and beguiled by the slots.

"You want to know the secret to a lifetime of successful gambling?" Rick asked. Slightly wary of being sold some kind of surefire system, I replied that I would like to know that secret.

"You gotta pace yourself, guy. If the Good Lord had wanted us to chase the dragon twenty-four–seven, he wouldn't have created golf courses."

Just then Rick's clubs showed up. He asked if I wanted to share a cab, and I agreed. I don't know why I agreed. If I was still in my New York mind-set I would have been profoundly suspicious of this slacker dude who chatted up strangers in the airport. But maybe my time in Ireland had tempered my cynicism and opened me up to meeting new people. Or maybe I was too tired and jet-lagged to worry about it. But the truth is that there's something about Rick that just makes you want to hang out with him. So I pointed my cart toward the blinding desert sun streaming through the exit doors and we headed outside.

Those of you who have never been to Las Vegas will not understand what I mean when I say that it is hot there. "What are you talking about?" you'll protest. "I know what 'hot' means. I live in Chicago (or Miami, or Caracas, or New Delhi)!" I don't care where you live. I don't care if you live on the surface of Mercury when it's at its closest point to the sun. Nothing and nowhere is as hot as Las Vegas in summer.

The reason that Las Vegas in summer is the hottest place in the universe is twofold. It's extremely hot. It's routinely 110 degrees. But far hotter than its mere hotness is the fact that the heat is exacerbated by the most staggeringly efficient air-conditioning system known to man. Most hot places have hot places, then some pretty hot places, then some warm places, then some coolish places, then a couple of cool areas, and maybe one really cold spot. Las Vegas is blazing hot everywhere except for everywhere else where it's fricking freezing. A hundred and ten degrees is always toasty. But after you've been playing blackjack in a meat locker for eight hours, 110 degrees suddenly feels like 910 degrees.

You know that tacky but ubiquitous Hollywood image of the supersexy femme fatale who is buck naked under her fur coat? Well, in Las Vegas that's actually a sensible outfit. Outside you'll wish you were naked. But you're gonna need the fur coat at every casino, strip club, steak joint, courthouse, and bowling alley in town.

As Rick and I cruised along in the taxi (approximate exterior temperature, 102 degrees; approximate interior temperature, 65 degrees), he told me a little about himself. He was a personal trainer based in New York. At least that was the job that paid for his health insurance, and provided a simple answer when people asked him what he did for a living. He made far more money gambling—primarily on sports, but he also played poker, blackjack, and craps. Roulette was for fun, special occasions, and whenever he was "really feeling it."

Far more than a personal trainer, or a gambler, Rick saw himself as a professional human being. It was a pretty short cab ride, but he was able to briefly sketch out his personal philosophy—and it sounded extremely appealing. He believed that most people just wanted to live a fun life. If they had a chance to do it again, they would prefer to live an interesting life. And if they got a final crack at it, they would choose to live a good life. But Rick was committed to doing all three at once.

I wanted to hear more about this bold plan. What exactly did it mean? What were the differences between "good," "interesting," and "fun" lives? Had he always lived this way, or was he—like me—trying out something new? Most importantly, I wanted to know if he had any success in implementing his philosophy? Lots of people talk the talk. But how was walking the walk working out?

Before he could answer any of these probing, and probably annoying, questions, Rick hopped out of the cab. We were at a red light on East Harmon, and he told me that he had $40,000 worth of winning tickets at the Planet Hollywood sports book.

"I gotta run, Bobby. Time to wake Vegas up and put her to work. See you around!"

He grabbed his golf clubs out of the trunk and jogged through the blistering heat toward a waiting bellboy. At the time it seemed odd that the only luggage with which he had come to Vegas was a set of golf clubs. But as I got to know Rick better, I stopped noticing little things like that.

We headed down Harmon and made a right. Suddenly, there in front of me, and behind me, and all around me was the Las Vegas Strip.

Okay, look—I know that as a New York–based, college-educated, pseudosophisticated, upwardly mobile urban professional (at least until a few months ago) I should view the Las Vegas Strip with scorn, condescension, and derision. It's tacky—I get it. It's shrill, and garish, and manipulative, and depressing, and it celebrates the worst qualities of capitalism and free-market economics. Yeah, whatever. All I really know is that when I made that right turn onto the Strip, and I saw that orgiastic explosion of neon and the seemingly endless row of massive, glitzy casinos, I was so damned thrilled that I had to sit on my hands to avoid clapping like a trained seal.

All that other stuff—the snobbishness and embarrassment—that's all learned behavior. We pick that up from the outside world like our teachers, or the *New York Times* op-ed page, or our (ex-)wives. But my stupid, shit-eating grin that simply would not leave my face for even a moment—that was real. That came from deep within my brain/heart/soul. And I was sick and tired of acting as if the things I just naturally liked (Vegas, beer, Dodger dogs, golf, Michael Bay movies) weren't "good" enough to really like. I was through with pretending that I preferred Twyla Tharp to *Saturday Night Fever*. As we pulled into the Bellagio's porte cochere, I gave up the fight altogether and actually started clapping like a trained seal.

The valet had clearly seen this kind of behavior many times before.

"Welcome to the Bellagio, sir. Will you be staying with us at the hotel?"

I nodded yes, gave him my last name, and arranged for the bags to meet me at check-in. Then I realized that a tip was probably in order. I have never been a good, natural tipper. I'm not cheap. I'm only too pleased to reward fine service generously. It's the actual handing over of the tip that I suck at. I always fumble for the money. Or I don't have the right bills and I'm embarrassed to ask for change. Or I don't know how to present the offer. Do I hold it out to him? Should I tuck it into his shirt pocket and then give it a pat like they would in *Goodfellas*? It's just something that never has come naturally to me.

But I was definitely going to tip this guy because he really had made me feel welcome. More importantly, I was hoping that a tip might get him to wish me luck. My already superstitious nature always kicked into hyperdrive whenever I was gambling. For some reason I decided that if this complete stranger in the cream-colored uniform and silly captain's hat would wish me luck, then I would have a great stay in Vegas.

I reached for my wallet and realized I was fishing in the wrong pocket. I found the right pocket but dropped my wallet as I pulled it out. Then I almost head-butted the valet like Giovanna as we both reached down to pick it up. Finally I tugged out a five-dollar bill and offered it up to him in the palm of both hands like a mental patient. Fortunately he acted as if this was all normal behavior. He took the bill and handed me my claim ticket as I walked away.

"Thank you, sir. And good luck!"

I swear to God—I almost went back and hugged him.

15

Here are the drawbacks to Las Vegas casinos: 1) People still smoke in them. 2) You can lose all of your money in them (plus money that you don't have but that your credit card companies will be only too glad to lend you).

Here are the good things about Las Vegas casinos: 1) Everything else.

I seriously cannot comprehend the inner workings of someone who claims not to like a Vegas casino. It's like hearing someone whine about having to breathe oxygen. And there are plenty of people like that out there. Not people who are oxygen whiners, casino complainers.

I guess I should be accepting of everyone's differences, but I truly don't understand why people dump on casinos. Sometimes I think that if money were never an issue, I would spend all my time in a nonstop gambling rush. But then I realize that the money is always an issue. That's a big part of the rush. If the money ceased being an issue, the fun might dissipate. I guess that's how guys like Charles Barkley end up in such hot water. Those who love to gamble will always push the stakes up until the threat of getting seriously hurt financially rears its ugly head. Those who have a real problem with gambling will not stop when the ugly head-rearing takes place.

While I don't understand the naysayers, I do understand the addicts. I know for a fact that I am not a gambling addict. I love doing it, it gives me a visceral thrill, and I have been known to bet over my head occasionally. But if I had to stop tomorrow, I could do it. No problem. I would miss it. But it doesn't control me.

I have felt the pull of it, though. And I have felt that stunned, heart-dropping feeling that comes after you've bet over your head and lost. I've noted the weird, powerless sensation you get when you realize you were just on the verge of being out of control. As if, for a brief moment, someone else had become the boss of your central nervous system and slid that stack of black chips onto twenty-nine. And I have been known to follow a bad bet with a worse bet in an attempt to win it all back, plus interest. This is what Rick calls "chasing the dragon." It can be fun, but you better be careful. Because dragons—while fictitious—are famous for eating people.

The human brain is weird. There are many complex scientific formulae and theories that doctors and researchers can spout about the brain, but none of them is going to be truer or more profound than that. Gambling is an activity that encourages the brain's weirdness to flourish. What is a rabbit's foot, or a lucky chip, or a sacred card protector other than a manifestation of the brain's bizarreness? We all know about statistics and probability. We all accept that the future has not been determined and cannot be influenced by the present. But if that's true, then why do we embrace silly talismans in an attempt to alter our luck? Why do we cross our fingers as the Hail Mary pass is in the air? Why do we bet our mother's birthday in the lottery? Why does my mind go through such tortured, pretzeled ramblings while the roulette wheel is spinning?

Here's a quick account of what goes through my head when I'm gambling. I jotted these notes down after one of my Vegas roulette sessions. Obviously, I have left out a billion thoughts that flew by too quickly to notate. But these are the biggies—the broad strokes—the feature film that was playing inside my cranium one afternoon at the Mirage moments after I eschewed my better judgment and slid that aforementioned stack of blacks onto twenty-nine.

First I think about how amazing it would be for twenty-nine to hit. As I start to calculate how much I'd win, another compartment in my brain starts berating me. "What the fuck are you doing?! You're jinxing yourself!" Properly admonished, I stop thinking about hitting my number. But then I start thinking that it's preposterous to stop thinking about hitting my number because my thoughts have absolutely no bearing on where that white ball lands. What possible difference could it make if I think about twenty-nine or not? But then I think that no one really knows that much about time. Didn't Einstein postulate that it's theoretically possible for the past and the future to exist simultaneously with the present? Or was that just some shitty movie I saw starring Dennis Quaid? Just to be safe, to hedge my bets, as it were, I decide to think about nothing at all. I will not jinx myself by being positive, nor will I jinx myself by being negative. I will outfox the fates by thinking nothing.

There's a moment where I am at peace and my brain is like a blank slate. But then I realize that thinking about thinking nothing at all is, quite obviously, thinking. Technically I was thinking about a blank slate, which made me think about chalk-boards, which made me think about high school chemistry, which made me think about petri dishes, which made me think about *The Dick Van Dyke Show*. The wheel and the ball are slowing down now and I'm starting to get desperate. I have to choose one thought and stick with it. I shuffle between around five hundred billion thoughts. For some reason I settle on Larry Johnson's four-point play for the Knicks in the 1999 playoffs. It was ridiculous. There was no way Antonio Davis fouled him during the shot—and I'm a Knicks fan! By the time the ball settles on fourteen, I'm lost in a sea of memories of LJ making that ridiculous *L* sign with his arms and wondering when we're ever going to make the playoffs again. By the time I realize that I have lost my entire stack of black chips, I barely have the energy to berate myself for not focusing hard enough on the task at hand.

They say that playing the stock market is exactly the same as gambling in a casino. But they are completely wrong. The actual gambling—the risking of one amount in the hopes of receiving a larger amount—that's the same. But the trappings that surround the gamble make a huge difference. On a basic level, almost everything is some kind of gamble—getting married, having kids, buying a house, eating sushi. You're laying out x for something that you hope will yield greater than x. But most other kinds of gambling are socially accepted. More than that, there's a whole other, more complex layer to the endeavor that's larger than the gambling aspect. Those other pursuits aren't defined by the gamble at their core. Stockbrokers put on suits and ties and take the 6 train to the office. They hide the gambling behind business, tradition, and custom.

It's not "normal" to consider your children to be a gamble. Most parents talk about playdates and SAT scores—not odds or returns. That said, when the guy across the street's kid gets into Cornell, he will walk around the neighborhood like he just hit the trifecta at Santa Anita.

Climbing Mount Everest or having unprotected sex in a tent in the Dutch countryside with some woman you just met at a bookstore aren't talked about as gambling either. There's a whole vocabulary for mountaineering or hooking up with backpackers that separates those acts from their essence of risk/reward.

But with gambling that veneer has been stripped away. The only concession to artifice is that chips take the place of real money. But trust me, if you insisted on only playing cash, you would always be able to find someone willing to handle your action.

I'm no longer even sure what point I'm trying to make. Gambling has a way of twisting the mind. I guess that's the point. Straight casino gambling is heady stuff. In some profound way it's more in tune with the core of being a socialized human being than playing the market, or having kids, or sleeping with Lowlanders. I can see how it could ruin people's lives if they're not equipped to handle it. I just can't see why other people—who are equipped to handle it—aren't interested in giving it a go.

Anyway, I wasn't thinking any of this as I walked into the Bellagio Hotel. I was thinking, "Holy shit! This place is like heaven on earth, if they filled heaven with sweaty, smoking sinners who use too much cologne." For those of you who have never been to the Bellagio, it's pretty much everything you expect a Vegas hotel to be. There are polished marble floors, and dancing water fountains, and a fancy modern art gallery, and an indoor botanical garden. There are five different pools, an enormous spa, a million restaurants and shops, an amphibious stage where crazy contorting Canadians gyrate on a nightly basis, and a gigantic Chihuly sculpture featuring thousands of glass flowers hanging from the ceiling—all attached to a huge casino.

Honestly, if I were designing paradise, I would use the Bellagio as a blueprint and then make some minor tweaks and adjustments from there. For example, I would definitely implement a no-smoking rule. And I might move the golf courses closer. But that's about it. I stood there in the lobby underneath those Chihuly flowers and I thought to myself, "How the hell does this Chihuly guy have time to make massive glass floral installations for every major hotel in the world? Doesn't he ever get stuck in traffic?" I consider my day well spent if I manage to get some letters in the mail and maybe change a lightbulb or two. That guy creates hundreds of cubic feet of top-notch art before breakfast.

But I didn't have time for jealousy or self-doubt. I had already heard the siren call of the casino. Those bells and chimes and clinks and clangs that drove Dostoyevsky to distraction were making me salivate like Charlie Sheen at a strip club. I wanted to dump my bags and hit the tables as soon as possible. Unfortunately, everyone else on the planet wanted the same thing. One thing about Las Vegas: every time I come here it has expanded exponentially in size. I have noticed literally two or three massive new hotels each time I arrive. And each time, everything is filled to capacity. It's as if it doesn't matter how big they make the town; it will always swell with hopeful tourists accordingly. And that's when it's over a hundred degrees outside. Can you imagine how popular this place would be if going outside didn't involve the possibility of bursting into flames?

I stood on line behind a sea of arriving tourists in order to check into my room. When I finally got to the front, I gave my name to the woman behind the desk. She punched some keys into the computer and announced that I was booked into one of their penthouse suites. She also suggested that if I needed any further assistance, I shouldn't hesitate to check in with the hotel's VIP services. She apologized profusely for having made me wait in this interminable line. I was liking the Bellagio more and more as she continued stroking me. Clearly my old Vegas client had taken care of me, but I wasn't exactly sure to what extent. I nervously asked the lady how much the rate on the room was going to be. She assured me that the hotel would be happy to comp me to a suite for as long as I would honor them with my presence. I was now liking the Bellagio as much as one can possibly like anything. I had reached the absolute peak on the like meter and was almost in need of switching over to the love gauge.

Thrilled, I headed off to the elevator bank to check out my new home for the next few months. I made a mental note to check in with my old client to ask him what kind of ridiculous lie he had fabricated in order to get me a free ride at the hotel. Was I supposed to pretend to be some dot-com whale eager to blow billions at the baccarat table? Did he tell them I was a Russian gangster laundering money earned selling illegal biological weapons to the Portuguese? Whatever it was, I was going to do my best to live up to it. I wasn't quite sure how I was going to convince anyone that I was a legit high roller, but I was willing to play whatever part I had to. Because I felt quite sure that I could definitely get used to the VIP lifestyle.

The bellboy accompanied me up to the thirtieth floor. I have never been in an elevator that moved so fast in all my life. It was almost the opposite experience to Colin's alcohol-fueled time travel. Instead of slowing things down, it seemed as if we magically teleported to the future. One moment we were in the lobby and the next we were on the top floor. It happened so quickly that it almost felt like we had arrived at the top floor *before* we had been in the lobby. In which case I guess we actually would have teleported to the past. Clearly, time was taking on a somewhat elastic quality during my travels. I decided not to mention any of this to the bellboy for fear that he might taser me repeatedly.

He led me to my suite, opened the door, and allowed me to enter first. I am not too proud to admit that when I saw the room, I almost started crying. And that was a pretty great feeling. Because I had done my fair share of crying recently and absolutely none of those tears had been tears of joy because I had just been comped to an unbelievable penthouse suite. They were mostly tears of sorrow that my wife was banging some guy named David. But that was in the past—like the magical elevator ride.

This hotel room wasn't just large, it was stupid large. It was crazy large. It was large and in charge. It was larger than my college dorm, my first apartment, and my second apartment all put together. And I'm pretty sure that neither my college dorm nor either of my first two apartments had two bedrooms, a massive wall of windows, a whirlpool bath, or a walk-in steam room. I would have remembered something like that.

I made a tight fist and dug my fingernails into my palm to avoid crying in front of the bellboy. I figured that ultra high rollers rarely wept in front of the hotel staff. It was now time to tip again. But I promised myself that there was not going to be a repeat performance of my embarrassing faltering tip with the valet. Since I was still operating under the assumption that I had to pretend to be some kind of big stakes player, I decided to tip the bellboy one hundred dollars. Somehow I managed to do this as if I had done it many times before—no dropped wallet or fumbling for bills or awkward exchanges. I just peeled off Ben Franklin and pressed him into my man's hand. I believe I actually said, "That's for you, kid." Dean Martin couldn't have tipped a bellboy with any more ease and style. I was already starting to relish my role as a player. The bellboy pocketed my C-note looking like a ten-year-old who just got a bicycle from Santa. He thanked me and insisted that if I needed anything at all I should ask for Paul. I assured him that I would. Paul left.

I pulled open the curtains and looked out over the dancing water fountains, past the Paris Hotel's Eiffel Tower, beyond the exploding volcano in front of the Mirage, and off into the distant mountain range. For a moment an intense feeling of satisfaction squeezed out every trace of the pain, rage, sadness, and disappointment with everything that had gone wrong with my life in New York. In another second, a lot of the misery squeezed back in. But just experiencing its absence for an instant filled me with hope for the future.

I kicked off my shoes and scrunched up my toes in the deep shag rug like John McClane in *Die Hard* (the first one). I popped the cork on my bottle of complimentary champagne the hotel had thoughtfully left on ice and took a swig right from the neck. I stared out at the city and toasted my reflection in the window. It's not often that a white man from Connecticut gets to say this, but I felt like I should be starring in a rap video.

Continuing with my newfound self-image as the star of my own glossy, Hollywood studio blockbuster, I decided to get a little exercise. I did a few deep knee bends to limber up the old joints. Then I dropped to the shag for some push-ups. I thought I'd do fifty because that seemed to be the default number of push-ups that guys do in the movies. At around number fourteen I started having severe doubts about the whole endeavor. I struggled to a shaky twenty and called it a day. I threw some water on my face, clapped my hands a little more like an ecstatic trained seal, and told my reflection that the time had come. I headed down to the casino. It was official: the Vegas portion of my yearlong journey of discovery and stupidity had begun.

16

When I told people that I was planning to disappear for the year and explore the world (or at least a few small slivers of it), they all had a lot of questions. To my surprise, the first question they asked was never "Why?" It was almost always "How are you going to pay for it?" I guess I should have been insulted that no one thought of me as a dashing, carefree millionaire who could effortlessly afford whatever capricious whim popped into my head. God knows there are a plenty of those guys in the ad business. I once worked for a company founded by a South African man who was so stupendously rich that he bought two Caribbean islands—one for his wife and one for his mistress. To his credit, the wife's island was larger—but the mistress's island was closer.

But I was not one of those guys. I had always worked hard and made decent money. But I couldn't afford to take a year off cruising around like a college kid whose daddy was paying for a semester at sea. I used that money I made to support myself and my wife in a style to which she became extremely accustomed.

Anything "extra" I would set aside and place in an investment or savings account. There wasn't a ton of extra money there, but over time it had built up respectably. There would be no Caribbean islands for anyone, but no one would be holding a fund-raiser for me either. I was never tempted to dip into my savings. They were clearly earmarked for a bold and brilliant—but completely undefined—future.

After my wife left me, I discovered that the future was now. Because within a week I began to notice that my financial ship had suddenly sprung a leak. My wife was taking money out of the extra accounts faster than I had ever put any in.

Ever since we met, I never begrudged her anything. From the first moment that we were together, I shared everything I had with her. Her name was on the deed to our apartment and our country house. She was even listed on the pink slip for my Volvo SUV, and she never even drove it. Her cars—the BMWs and then, after her semispiritual awakening, her Toyota Prius—were always hers and hers alone (even though I paid for them). She also had unlimited and equal access to all of our funds. I never took exception to the fact that I would work hard, save, and invest—and then she would go to Canyon Ranch with her friends for a week and gut punch our credit cards. I never fought with her about money once. And it wasn't like I wasn't concerned sometimes. Just knowing that she was burning big bills at a luxury spa made me nervous. I would walk to work and eat ramen for dinner hoping to offset the expenditures in some small way. But I never held that against her or threw it in her face.

When I saw what she was up to after she left, however, my mind-set shifted slightly. There was no way I was going to sit idly by and let her spend all the money I'd made while she rode David's baloney pony. What the hell did she suddenly need twenty-five thousand dollars for? A titanium broom and platinum pointy witch's hat? I couldn't believe that she was doing this to me. I felt like a character in an especially crappy John Updike short story. Well, I wasn't going to take it any longer. I decided that it would be duplicitous (and possibly illegal) to suddenly shift the money to a different account with just my name on it. But I felt it would be the very essence of justice to withdraw as much cash as I could get my hands on and use it to fund my fun.

So the answer to the question "how could I afford my travels?" is that I couldn't. I could pay for them only because I was blowing all the money that I had set aside for my future to enjoy my present. Just like Albert Brooks in *Lost in America,* I now found myself in Las Vegas gambling my nest egg. Of course, I had already been in Ireland drinking my nest egg. At least in Vegas I had an outside shot of getting some of it back. So between my wife siphoning the accounts and my harebrained scheme to drop out of the rat race, my savings were disappearing quickly. When you consider that I had quit my job and was now an aging, slightly unbalanced advertising executive in a world that probably didn't even need young, totally balanced advertising executives, you may begin to realize what a precarious position I was in.

But as I took the world's fastest elevator down to the casino floor, I wasn't even remotely concerned about any of that. I had five thousand dollars in cash in my pocket, Elvis Presley's "Viva Las Vegas" blasting in my brainpan, and I was ready to give the Bellagio the beating of a lifetime.

The elevator doors opened and I allowed the sights and sounds of a first-class casino in full swing to wash over me.

Here's a partial list of what I took in during my first moments out on the casino floor:

An old, obese lady with prodigious rolls of neck fat, wearing a green-on-green pantsuit, sitting on a bright red motorized scooter, was pressing the "max credits" button on a slot machine over and over without ever looking up, without ever touching the cigarette that dangled from her lips and was growing desperately close to burning her face, and without ever hitting a single payout in the entire time I watched her (about three minutes).

All I heard was an absolute wall of sound. Phil Spector would have been impressed (if he weren't so deranged). I could not pick up a scintilla of silence anywhere in the dense aural tapestry of ringing bells, clinking coins, piped-in music, joyful shrieks, and desperate wails.

A tall, thin cowboy-looking guy with a sleeveless Harley-Davidson T-shirt and faded jeans sat down at a nearby roulette table and placed four purple ($500) chips in front of him. He bet them each, one by one, on black. Red hit three times. Then double-zero (green) hit. The tall man stood up and reached into his pocket. I thought it was fifty-fifty that he was going for either more chips or a pistol. Instead he pulled out a five-dollar bill, tossed it to the dealer, and walked away. He never said a word to anyone.

Three thick-necked, twenty-something guys wearing khaki shorts, sweatshirts, and baseball caps with various team logos on them were heading toward the exit. The one on the right was jokingly telling everyone in front of him to step aside. The one in the middle was grinning widely.

The one on the left was pounding the one in the middle on the back with an open palm. He was yelling the following: "That was the sickest shit I ever saw, bro!" He said this at least three times. They left the casino. I do not know what "sick shit" he was referring to.

A young boy who looked to be around eight years old wandered down a carpeted path that led through a block of slot machines toward the table games. He was staring at the ceiling (which, in his defense, was pretty impressive, filled as it was with "eyes in the sky"). After a moment a woman who must have been his mother grabbed him by the arm and slapped his face. "You can't be over here, Devin! I told you to wait by the fountain." Before the boy could explain himself, the woman asked if he'd spent his ice cream money. Devin hadn't—which was too bad because the woman demanded it back and sent him off to wait at the fountain again. I did not stick around long enough to find out whether or not the ice cream money bore fruit.

At the same time that the thin cowboy got felted, a stunning young Asian woman with an Asian boyfriend wearing a polo shirt with the collar popped hit the double-zero hard. She had around twenty five-dollar chips that paid off to varying degrees. Her total bet of $100 must have yielded at least $1,500. I don't think she quite understood what had happened when her number hit. But, as the dealer slid the large ziggurat of chips she just won toward her, she let out one of the six most lengthy and piercing screams that I have ever heard in my life. If she ever wins the Super Lotto, I'm sure everyone in the galaxy will know about it instantaneously.

These vignettes are merely momentary observations. If I had taken a photograph of the scene at the far edge of the casino closest to the elevator banks, I'm sure I could describe fifty other moments like these. There's always something happening on the floor. And always is in no way hyperbolic. There's never nothing going on in a Vegas casino. At every second of every day, at least one person is gambling somewhere in every casino. I have no facts to back this up, but I'd lay ten to one that it's true. There really aren't any mirrors at casinos. And there are no clocks. And I wouldn't be surprised if they pump in pure oxygen, as some people have suggested. The casino bosses don't want anyone to see how haggard they really look, or know what time it is, or get too sleepy. They want you chasing that dragon at all times and they'll do everything in their power to keep the chase going twenty-four hours a day.

As it turns out, they don't really have to do too much in their power. The absence of mirrors and clocks does the trick for me. When I've got a good gambling vibe going I lose all sense of time within about fifteen minutes. If the tables are running hot, what difference does it make if it's four in the afternoon or four in the morning? It's not like I have to get to work. When I was in Vegas, I became a vampire. I gambled instead of drinking blood. And instead of avoiding sunlight, I avoided ever not being inside a casino. When the time came where I could no longer avoid the overwhelming need to rest, I would repair to my two-bedroom penthouse coffin and grab some shut-eye.

But this first moment on the floor wasn't about rest, it was about kicking off the action with a bang. I could already see what Rick had meant about playing the slots at the airport. I felt like a moron for wasting all that time that could now still be stretching out before me—so that I could waste it here.

What should my first move be? High-stakes roulette? Should I navigate the mysterious waters of Caribbean stud? Perhaps a visit to the Orient with some Pai Gow poker?

But then it was as if the skies parted and the sun shone down on a newly vacated seat at a twenty-five-dollar-minimum blackjack table. The assembled players looked like a hearty bunch of good-natured scoundrels. The dealer seemed an honest soul—as dedicated to making me a winner as I was to not letting him down. As I drew near, I noticed that his name tag read, "Onald." I don't know why I took this as a good sign, as opposed to an obvious typo.

"Mind if I play in midshoe?" I asked the others at the table. Usually it's considered poor form to start playing blackjack before the dealer finishes the deal, shuffles the cards, and sets up a new shoe. I guess some people think that it throws the luck out of whack. So I always ask. The last thing I want is some angry Korean grandmother giving me the stink eye all night because she thinks I stole her queen of diamonds. But everyone encouraged me to hop right in. As Onald converted my initial $500 offering into twenty green $25 chips, he wished me good luck.

"Onald," I said. "If I win big tonight, I'm going to buy you an *R* for your first name."

Onald looked at me without any reaction whatsoever. I think he was from the Philippines so it's possible that he didn't understand my attempt at humor. Of course, it's far more possible that it just wasn't funny. But my philosophy of talking to dealers is that it's not always so important to be funny. The important thing is to say completely crazy things and to never stop saying them.

Gambling has a lousy reputation as a silent, introspective, solitary, and selfish pursuit. This couldn't be further from the truth. The truth is that talking really is one of the most fun parts about gambling in a casino. Playing these games loosens the tongue for almost everyone. The free cocktails also help. But there's an openness of exchange that happens at a casino that doesn't happen everywhere. Complete strangers high-five each other when the dealer busts or someone hits a twenty-one. Deranged shouting, howling, singing, joking, and pleading isn't just tolerated—it's encouraged. Craps players holler at the dice, pleading for them to land on "puppy's paws" (two fives). When the dealer shows sixteen and takes a card, seemingly mild-mannered housewives shriek at him to "Break! Break, damn you!" When high rollers are placing hundred-dollar bets at roulette, they've been known to exhort the dealers to "Hit them cupcakes with some chocolate sprinkles, baby!"

When I went to work in New York City every morning, and when I came home every afternoon, I must have passed a total of at least one million people. I never said a word to any of them. But five minutes in a casino and I'm best friends with the dude from Senegal sitting to my right. And I'm asking the pit boss about where's the best place to buy some pork chops at five in the morning. We may never see each other again, but while we're shoulder to shoulder playing hard, we're sharing something real.

Playing at a casino is a lot like drinking in a good Irish pub that way. The chips and the beer, the money and the whiskey are almost beside the point. Sure, we wouldn't be there if it weren't for the chips, the beer, the money, and the whiskey, but the reason we keep coming back—the reason we stay so long—is because we're all having such a goddamned good time together. That's why I never got seduced by online gambling. If I wanted to make money depressed and alone staring at a computer monitor all day, I'd just go to the office.

I start my Las Vegas casino gambling sojourn small. I bet the table minimum, twenty-five dollars. My first two cards are a nine and a three. The dealer shows a two. I'm a big believer in "the book." I've never actually read the book. I don't even know if there really is a book. There are probably thousands of them, all completely contradictory. But over the years I have internalized certain rules for all these different games. And, in my heart of hearts, these rules compromise the book. They're what you're "supposed" to do. And in my book, you always hit a twelve once—and only once—when the dealer shows a two. I have never bothered to learn whether or not there is any mathematical validity to this technique. But you simply don't mess with the book.

Onald peels off a three for me, and I wave him off telling him I'm going to stand pat. Onald flips up his hole card—a ten of clubs. As he reaches for the next card out of the shoe, I shout out a well-meaning "Over the falls, Onald!" Onald deals himself a Jack of diamonds. He has a twenty-two. He has busted. He has indeed gone over the falls. There is some small rejoicing at the table as Onald pays us out. He places a new green twenty-five-dollar chip next to the original twenty-five-dollar chip that I just bet.

I have just doubled my money in Vegas. Life is good.

I decide to play what I like to call a modified Kogen. This is a system of betting that probably makes no sense whatso-ever but one that I think I heard about from someone who seemed to know what he was talking about. The nuts and bolts of it are as follows: if I win three hands in a row, I double my bet. If I lose a hand, I scale back all the way down to my original bet. And that's the modified Kogen. So, after that initial twenty-five-dollar win, I pulled the winnings off the table and risked my initial twenty-five again. I won. Then I won for a third time, so I pumped my bet up to fifty dollars. I won again.

On the next hand, Lady Luck saw fit to bestow upon me a blackjack featuring a luscious queen of hearts and an elegant ace of spades. I was now up two hundred dollars. Although if I counted my losses at the airport, I was actually down one hundred dollars overall. I decided that I better cut that shit out. If I was going to spend four months in Vegas, there was no way I could keep a constant running count of how much I was up or down. I was just going to play and have fun. I'd worry about profit or loss at a later date. Besides, the actual numerical amount you are up or down has very little to do with whether or not you're a winner in Vegas.

We're now heading into an extremely complex and theoretical discussion about abstract mathematics. I like to call it "Vegas math." There are plenty of brilliant math geniuses in the casinos of Las Vegas. Guys like Chris "Jesus" Ferguson and Phil "The Poker Brat" Hellmuth can compute the odds of winning a pot or pulling a two-outer to make the nut flush in a heartbeat. But that's not the kind of math I'm talking about. You don't have to be a genius to grasp "Vegas math." Here— I'll break it down for you.

Say you went to Vegas with $3,000. You lost it all, and then you withdrew another $1,000 as a cash advance on one of your credit cards. You blew $850 of that. You probably would have gambled away your last $150, but you were late for your flight home and your friends forced you to leave. According to conventional math, you lost $3,850 (plus the interest you're being charged by those bloodsuckers at your credit card company who really nail you for those cash advances).

But according to Vegas math those numbers are very different. Sure, you lost $3,850. But how much fun did you have?

Did you get comped to go see *O*? You did, didn't you? And it kicked ass, right? And how about those steaks for dinner on Tuesday? They were awesome! And then when you and your buddies got wrecked and Josh tried to jump across the canal at the Venetian? That was hilarious! And what about that smoking hot chick who grabbed your ass when you asked her to blow on your dice? How much was *that* worth? Well, I'll tell you how much: $12,000. That's right—according to my calculations, you had $12,000 worth of fun. So when we subtract $3,850 from that we discover that you went to Las Vegas and you actually *won* $8,150! Congratulations!

Strangely there is no converse corollary to Vegas math. If you actually won $12,000 at a poker tournament, but you had a really shitty time, then you still won $12,000. I'm telling you—it's a wonderful place.

I kept my hot streak going at Onald's blackjack table for a few hours. Even though they kept filtering in new dealers, I still thought of the table as Onald's. And every time he shifted back in, I would great him like a long-lost brother—from the Philippines. My modified Kogen did me proud. I got up to betting two hundred dollars a hand three different times. By the end of the night when I was too exhausted and jet-lagged to think straight, I had a nice stack of greens and blacks in front of me. I thanked my fellow players and wished them a good evening. Then I tipped Onald some chocolate (a black one-hundred-dollar chip) and asked him to color me up. He thanked me and slid back a respectable stack of purple five-hundred-dollar chips, which I shoved in my pockets.

The hypervator hurled me back to my penthouse suite and I tumbled into my giant and supremely comfortable bed. I knew that there would be many more twists and turns in my upcoming journey—some would be good, some would probably suck. But day one in Las Vegas had been about as great as I ever could have imagined. I had to just enjoy the good, and I'd deal with the sucky if and when it happened. As my head hit the pillow, I was surprised to find myself thinking about Alicia. She seemed like the kind of person who would have gotten a real kick out of a day like today. But why the hell was I thinking about her? I barely knew the woman. I never even got her phone number or her e-mail address. What an idiot. I should have asked for her card. Fortunately, I was too tired and too content to beat myself up about it. I pushed her out of my mind. After all, I'd never see her again. "Today was a good day," I told myself as Elvis Presley continued to sing "Viva Las Vegas" in my brain. I closed my eyes and slept the sleep of the innocent, the lucky, and the happy.

17

The next day I got demolished.

Everything started out as wonderfully as the previous day had ended. I got up around noon in total darkness. All I heard was the low, steady whirr of the air-conditioning unit, which was maintaining the interior temperature of my suite at a delectable sixty-eight degrees. I'm sure that I was single-handedly deforesting at least an acre of rain forest, but when it comes to AC I'm not a tree hugger, I'm a Bush hugger. Call me a Neanderthal reactionary, but I consider conditioned air to be one of my inalienable rights. I'll bring my own fabric bag to the supermarket, and I can recycle with the best of them—but I will not forsake the Freon-cooled air that made this country great.

As for the darkness, it is a greatly appreciated mystery whose secrets are known only by good hotels. Why is it that you can achieve total obscurity only in a hotel room? Every bedroom that I have ever had in every dorm, apartment, or house has had myriad openings through which the sun would creep. And it wasn't like I didn't fight the good fight. I installed blinds, curtains, and blackout shades. I even tried taping them to the glass like the nutjob in *Insomnia*. But the sunlight would always beat me. Somehow, though, the good folks at the Bellagio had been able to hermetically seal out the light. At four in the afternoon, with the Vegas sun blazing outside like a thousand exploding stars, I could make my suite blacker that the darkest corner of the Luray Caverns just by closing the drapes.

I woke up and took a shower in an enclosure large enough to raise cattle. There were more nozzles in that thing than in a fire truck. I had jets of water shooting up, out, over, around, and through my body. By the time I was finished, my spleen was clean. I threw on some clothes, grabbed a nice, ripe nectarine out of the complimentary fruit basket that the hotel had provided, shoved last night's purples in my pocket, and headed down to the casino.

My first stop was last night's blackjack table. Onald was not there. A middle-aged Asian woman named Say was working the felt. The table was empty except for an obscenely large sweaty man wearing a Green Bay Packers cap sitting in the anchor seat. I asked him if he minded if I played in the middle of the shoe. His response was, "Fuckin' A, I mind." Nonplussed, I sat down and waited for the shoe to turn over. I probably should have left right there. It can't be good hoodoo to play cards with some creepy giant who smells like wet cheese and has already been rude to me. But I figured that last night's good luck would overwhelm today's bad luck.

I was wrong.

Right from the first hand, Say started whacking me. And she wouldn't do it nicely. It's one thing when you've got a fifteen and the dealer's showing a ten. You hit, bust, and lose the hand. I can deal with that. But it's very painful when you've got a nineteen and the dealer's showing a four. She turns over the hole card to reveal a ten. Then she pulls an ace, another ace, and then a five to crush your spirit with an unanticipated five-card Charlie. When she does this over and over again, you start to take it personally.

The other thing you start to do is chase the dragon. This is the opposite of the modified Kogen. Instead of implementing and sticking with a controlled betting strategy, chasing the dragon means risking more and more money in a desperate attempt to retrieve what you've already lost. Frequently chasing the dragon is accompanied by clammy palms, a sinking feeling in the pit of your stomach, and extreme light-headedness.

After I lost my first purple, I also lost my self-control. I started using Vegas math for evil instead of for good. I figured that if I had just lost four hands in a row, then the next hand was bound to be a winner, so I should bet five times the amount I'd normally bet, and then I'd be even. After this didn't work twice, I decided that I was being punished for thinking small. Why was I worried about breaking even? I was at the tables to give this casino a beating. Forget five times the amount I'd normally bet, it was time to play some purple.

I placed my $500 chip in the betting circle and received two eights. The dealer was showing a six. For a moment I wondered whether or not I should really split those eights. The book demanded it, but I'd be risking a grand on one hand. Then I chastised myself for ever doubting the sanctity of the book. I placed another purple chip next to the first one and told Say to split 'em. She filled up each hand with a glorious face card. Now, I had two eighteens against her six. She flipped her down card up to reveal a ten of clubs. Then she pulled a four off the deck and swept away my thousand dollars.

For some reason the sweaty giant in the anchor seat chose this moment to call me a "fucking douche bag." I don't know if he was angry because I had queered his luck or because he thought I was playing poorly. I prefer to think that he was merely an extremely perceptive man with a foul mouth. Because right then I really felt like a fucking douche bag. I had blown through around six thousand dollars in less than an hour. And I wasn't even enjoying myself. Actually, I kind of felt like I was having a stroke. Mercifully, the yellow cut card popped up and Say had to roll over a new shoe. I mustered what little physical strength I had left and was able to push myself away from the table. I wished Say and the rude behemoth a lovely afternoon and stumbled away in a daze.

My intention was to return to my suite, close the blinds to convert the space into a massive sensory deprivation chamber, and cry myself back to sleep. But the flesh is weak, and my brain is even weaker. As I walked toward the elevator bank I came across a $500 chip wedged deep in my pocket that I hadn't noticed earlier. This was a gift from the gods—I wasn't busted after all. I weathered the storm of defeat and humiliation and was still walking away with a little something to show for my efforts. Unfortunately I was walking away right next to a roulette wheel.

My heart leapt. Here was my chance to win it all back in one shot! But my brain was having none of it. I knew how bad it would feel to lose it all moments after I'd already thought I'd lost it all. But I did have to admit that it would feel amazing to get back in the black after the beating I just took. I made a small gentleman's wager with myself. If the current spin landed on black, then I'd play. Red, I'd walk away. Double-zero hit. Neither red nor black, this result placed me in a quandary. I solved the quandary by saying, "Ah, what the hell. I got more money upstairs." I asked the dealer if I could play my purple chip. He checked with the pit boss who okayed the bet. Five hundred dollars turned out to be the maximum bet allowable on any individual number at the current gaming stakes at this table.

I had never bet the limit before and my heart insisted that the time was right. I was no longer listening to my brain. I think my brain may have even been caught up in the excitement by now. If we hit the winning number with this bet, we'd win $17,500. Plus the half dozen people sitting around the table would think I was a superstar. Granted, I'd never see any of them again. But just knowing that some complete strangers out there would be pressing license plates or serving frozen yogurt while fondly recalling the time when that guy hit his number on a max bet made me feel like a winner.

But where to place my chip? Obviously I could have broken it down into smaller denominations. This was a $10 table, which meant that everyone had to be risking a total of at least $10 on every spin of the wheel. I could have changed my purple into five hundred one-dollar chips. Properly spread out, that could have lasted me for an hour—even if I never won a single spin. But I was already committed to letting it ride. I surveyed the numbers and did a quick analysis of each. Surprisingly my emotions had a lot to do with the choice.

My birthday was on the twenty-fifth, but that seemed a little trite. My basketball number in high school was thirty-one, but that was also my wife's birthday—so that wasn't happening. Every number I looked at triggered both positive and negative thoughts. Twelve? Sure, I was spending twelve months on the road during my journey. But twelve was also Tom Brady's number and I can't stand him. What a loser move—leaving Bridget Moynihan for Gisele Bundchen. Four? Four used to be my favorite number, but it's left a bad taste in my mouth ever since the Red Sox won four in a row from the Yankees back in 2004. (Even though I was born and raised in Connecticut, I've always been a New York sports fan. For better or worse, this fact has colored many of my decisions.)

Then I noticed twenty-nine. Black twenty-nine. I couldn't think of any twenty-nines in my life. Nothing good popped up, nothing bad came to mind. Twenty-nine seemed totally neutral. So, twenty-nine it was. I shoved the purple chip on top of that number just before the dealer waved his arm over the table and announced, "No more bets."

At this point my brainpan became a theater in the round for every lunatic idea, superstition, and wish I'd ever had. A billion thoughts exploded at once. Part of me was actively and desperately wishing for twenty-nine to hit. Part of me was honestly wondering if my wanting the number to hit could possibly impact that number hitting. Part of me was telling other parts of me to calm down and be quiet. And another part of me was aware that everyone else at the table was probably having this exact same cavalcade of craziness swirling around in their heads.

The wheel and the ball slowed down in their opposite arcs. The ball started skipping and bouncing from number to number. The ball settled in twenty-nine. An intense roar of exhilaration started forming in my shoes and working its way up my legs. The ball teetered out of twenty-nine and landed permanently on the adjacent number. Twenty-five.

"Twenty-five! Red! No winners!"

The dealer raked away all the chips. I sat there staring at the winning number, still spinning softly, in disbelief. Twenty-five.

Of course it was twenty-five! There's a reason that betting your birthday is trite and a cliché. Because, like all trite clichés, it's based on the truth! You always bet your birthday! What the hell had I been thinking? Isn't gambling just like the SATs? Aren't you always supposed to go with your first instincts?

I could no longer live with this shame in public. I was convinced that all those people who moments ago were going to be wistfully recalling my winning play while tromping through their dead-end lives would now be laughing at my failure while jet-setting around the French Riviera. The woman sitting to my immediate left was around fifty years old. She appeared to be from Southeast Asia and was eating some noodles out of a Tupperware container that she had clearly brought with her to the casino. She had twenty-seven dollars in front of her, some slightly soiled Kleenex, and had been nursing the same complimentary gin and tonic for the past half hour. The likelihood that this person would soon be chortling at my expense while speedboating with Prince Albert of Monaco was, realistically, extremely slim. But at that moment, I could actually hear her telling Albert the story of my defeat and shame. She called him Al—and the son of a bitch laughed uproariously while the choppy waves sprayed sea foam on top of his big bald head.

Disgusted with myself, I stormed back up to my suite, closed the blinds, and hurled myself into bed.

18

Not surprisingly, I couldn't sleep. First of all, I'd just woken up a few hours earlier. Secondly, I was so jacked up on adrenaline that I kept replaying the various hands that Say murdered me with over and over again. Every time I shut my eyes I saw that damn ball skipping out of twenty-nine and landing on twenty-five. The perverse bad luck that had plagued me at blackjack destroyed me at roulette. Like I said, it's one thing to just lose. But when you lose in such a cruel way—with winning so tantalizingly close—it eats away at you.

I had to do something or I'd go nuts. But what do you do in Vegas if you're too nut-punched to gamble? It was too early to catch the Amazing Jonathan—besides, I hate magic acts. So I decided to go to the gym.

There are only two kinds of people who go to the gym in Las Vegas: people who hate gambling and people who have just taken a beating at the tables. Since people who hate gambling rarely go to Las Vegas, the gyms there are pretty much filled with losers. And I'm not making a moral judgment about these people. As I approached an open treadmill, I was most emphatically one of them.

It was a pretty depressing exercise session. Since I was sure that the story of my ruinous run had spread across the town by now, I avoided direct eye contact with everyone. I just jogged along with my headphones on, staring at the plasma screen playing SportsCenter but not really watching or listening.

My mind was reeling. I was supposed to be in Vegas for four months. I was supposed to have all kinds of fun in Vegas for four months. But so far I had been in Vegas for twenty-four hours and I had already experienced a soul-crushing reversal of fortune at the tables. If I blew all of the money I'd brought with me in the first week, what the hell was I supposed to do for the rest of the time?

I forgot to mention something earlier when I was describing Vegas math. The mathematical coefficient that is the key to having fun in Las Vegas, regardless of how much you lose, is always having money when you're in Las Vegas. You don't have to have a lot. But you have to have some. When you have no money in Las Vegas, and you can't get any more out of your ATM, and your credit cards are all maxed out, and your buddies no longer think of you as a reliable credit risk, then there's only one thing to do: leave Las Vegas.

But I was committed to staying here for the long haul. So what was I going to do if I kept getting wiped out? I was really stressing over this as I was pounding the treadmill. Maybe I should have stayed in Ireland. Maybe I should never have even started this stupid trip. Maybe I should go back to New York and beg for my old job back. If the purpose of this whole expedition was to have fun, then things had really started going off the rails. Because I wasn't just not having fun. Now I was not having fun *and I was jogging*. I hate jogging. A lot. On an average day, I would honestly rather get hit in the shins (lightly) by a hammer than jog more than a block or two. But here I was humping along this stupid treadmill worrying about my future. The situation was getting dangerous—I was really starting to doubt myself.

That's when I felt a tap on my shoulder. I turned around and there was Rick jogging along on the treadmill next to me. He said something, but I still had the headphones on and couldn't hear. I removed the headphones. He repeated what he'd said before.

"Take a beating, huh?"

Shit. Everyone *was* talking about it.

"Who told you?" I asked him.

"No one had to tell me. The only people jogging at two in the afternoon at the Bellagio gym are people who just took a beating."

"I guess that means you took a beating too."

"No, man," he said. "I work here sometimes as a personal trainer. I just finished up an hour with Deepak Chopra and now I'm cooling down. By the way, you'll get better cardio if you breathe in through your nose and out through your mouth."

I don't know what surprised me more—that Deepak Chopra has a personal trainer, that I now knew Deepak Chopra's personal trainer, or that Deepak Chopra was currently in Las Vegas. I would have figured that he'd be somewhere classy and spiritual, like Italy, India, or—I don't know—Bali, maybe.

Rick wanted to know what had happened, so I told him about my brutal day so far.

"And *that's* what's got you in the gym? That's what you're all stressed out about?"

I explained how it was kind of eating away at me and making me doubt my whole extended Vegas plan. Rick just shook his head.

"You need a significant attitude adjustment. You want to grab some lunch?"

I told him that it sounded like a good idea.

He hopped off the treadmill, completely unfazed by the run. I, on the other hand, was about to puke. Trying to keep pace with Rick while maintaining a conversation at the same time almost killed me. But I didn't want Rick to see me in my weakened condition so I pretended to tie my shoes for about two minutes while I caught my breath.

Rick chuckled at my sorry state and playfully snapped a towel at me. He told me to raise my arms above my head, and to walk it out. Then he told me to meet him downstairs at Prime in ten minutes.

I crouched there for a moment feeling like a total dork as I wheezed desperately with both arms stretched toward the heavens. I heard someone pass by and say, "That Rick is a real killer, huh?"

I looked up just in time to watch Deepak leave the gym.

When I got down to the restaurant, Rick was already at the table. In fact, he was the only person at any table. He had showered and changed, ordered a pitcher of Arnold Palmers, and was busy chatting up an extremely pretty waitress.

"Bobby! Have a seat. Stella, this is my friend Bobby. He got whacked this morning, and I think that nothing short of a porterhouse is going to make him feel better."

Stella hurried off to place our order.

I turned to Rick. "I thought this place is only open for dinner."

"It is," he replied. "But I train Jean-Georges so they take care of me here. They also never charge me, so relax and enjoy."

And that's exactly what I did. The steak was excellent. The company was agreeable. Stella was adorable. She was the first person I ever met in my entire life who was actually from Las Vegas. Like—originally. She didn't come to visit and end up staying there. She was born there. Until that moment I had never entertained the possibility that normal American lives were unfolding in that part of the desert. It seemed impossible that within a few blocks of these mammoth casinos, husbands and wives were serving their kids macaroni and cheese. How could Mike "The Mouth" Matusow suck out on the river to scoop a $300,000 pot from Daniel "Kid Poker" Negreanu in the same zip code where seventh graders were learning about the Protestant Reformation and wondering where babies come from?

Obviously, I'm an idiot. I don't know why I was surprised to hear about Stella's background. Vegas is a huge city with all the same boring stuff that all huge cities have. Movie theaters, hospitals, schools, churches, and an enormous casino/hotel tower that features a giant teeter-totter that whips you in circles while you're suspended nine hundred feet above the ground. You know—just like where you live.

While we ate, Rick heard my whole sorry tale. The big breakup, my mini breakdown, my time in Ireland, and my plans for the year.

Rick was a big fan of the whole idea. He had kind of dedicated his entire life to the spirit of what I was doing for these twelve months. He's extremely smart and well educated and has held a variety of impressive jobs in challenging careers. But he never allowed them to hem him in. He's been a practicing lawyer, a respected teacher, and a successful investor, but he insists that his job as a personal trainer has given him more freedom, fun, and entertainment than all of those other jobs put together.

"You've got a great opportunity here, Bobby. Most people just go though their lives complaining that they never have any fun. You've actually put yourself out there on the front lines and you're looking for the action. That's awesome!"

I agreed that in principle it was awesome. But right now it wasn't feeling so awesome. I had come to Vegas looking for adventure and had already gotten my ass handed to me at the tables.

"Give me a break," he answered. "First of all, adventure doesn't mean smiles, balloons, and handshakes. Sometimes getting your ass handed to you can be one hell of an adventure. And what did I tell you yesterday in the cab? You gotta pace yourself, remember? Life isn't a sprint, brother. It's a marathon—but not a grueling marathon where you cramp up and lose control of your bowels. It's a nice long, leisurely jog through experiences and relationships and a lot of fun and a little heartbreak, with the occasional balls-out sprint thrown in there for good measure."

I could see his point, but I had paced myself for my entire adult life, and where had it gotten me?

Rick said, "There's a difference between pacing yourself and running in place. But maybe I should show you what I mean. I've got a feeling that I'm talking to a fellow golfer, right?"

I assured him that he was indeed talking to a fellow golfer. Along with drinking and gambling, playing golf was one of my top three things to do with every second of every day.

"All right then," he said. "I'm going to show you how to do Vegas right. Let's hit the links."

19

Let me say a few words about how I feel about golf. I love golf. That's it in a nutshell. I love golf. I don't know if I need to elaborate upon that sentiment, but I will.

I love the feeling that vibrates up from my hands, through my arms, and into my whole body when I hit a ball just right. I love the sound that a well-struck ball makes. I love the sound that a poorly struck ball makes. I love the smell of the cut grass. I love the smell of the hot dogs spinning in that weird rotisserie thing at the snack shack. I love not knowing how I'm going to play from one minute to the next. I love being outdoors. I love wearing the soft spikes and seeing the starlike indentations they leave in the grass. I love all the ridiculous rules and the fact that I have to enforce them all on myself. I love that some people think playing golf an elitist waste of time but I know how good it makes me feel inside and out. I love hitting a perfect pitching wedge and sticking it five feet from the hole. I even love shanking a four iron and watching it skip halfway across a lake. I love the caddies and the golf carts and the clubhouses and the shining pyramids of freshly washed balls stacked up for me on the range. I love playing a really crappy golf course, in the rain, when I have blisters on my hands and feet, and I'm playing horribly, and I'm losing money to three obnoxious jerks that the starter forced me to play with.

So you can just imagine how much I loved that round with Rick.

Rick drove us out of town toward the mountains. He clearly no longer needed me to spring for a cab ride as somehow, somewhere, he had gotten his hands on an extremely lovely vintage Jaguar convertible. His sticks were in back and he told me that he had arranged for a set to be waiting for me at the club. I asked him where we were playing and he informed me that it was a nice track and he hoped I liked it.

Then he pulled up at the bag drop at Shadow Creek. I had to stop myself from screaming like those teenage girls did when the Beatles got off the plane at Idlewild.

Shadow Creek is ridiculous. It was originally built by re- nowned course architect Tom Fazio for mega-quadrillionaire Steve Wynn. For a long time it was Wynn's personal golf course. There were no memberships. Only Steve and the people he invited ever played it. He had moved tons of earth to create grassy berms all around the perimeter so that no one could see in. Then he imported all kinds of amazing flora and fauna to make the place completely unique. There are actual Australian wallabies living there. Wallabies! In Nevada!

More recently, the course has been opened up to the guests of Wynn's hotels in Las Vegas. But they still have to shell out five hundred dollars for one round on the glorious green. I had always heard about Shadow Creek but never expected to play there. As a guest of the Bellagio, I was allowed to play there—the thought of actually playing there just never entered my mind. It would be like some goofy kid throwing a ball around in the park suddenly standing on the mound at Yankee Stadium.

I asked Rick if he was sure about this. I hadn't played in over a year. I was too busy drinking in Ireland—although God knows they have some staggeringly beautiful golf courses there too. And before that I was too depressed lugging around the decaying corpse of my marriage to hit the links.

Rick assured me that this was going to be just what I needed. He also told me not to worry about the five hundred bucks. This round was on the arm.

"Seriously?" I asked. "Why? Are you Steve Wynn's personal trainer too?"

"No," he replied. "I saved his life once when we were heli-skiing in New Zealand."

I was beginning to discover that Rick was a man of many mysteries. Or he was an incredibly good liar. After all, I was pretty sure that Steve Wynn was legally blind. What the hell was he doing heli-skiing? Or was I just being prejudiced and small-minded assuming that the sightless shouldn't be allowed to heli-ski? Whichever way it turned out—that Rick was a true Renaissance man or a true bullshit artist—at that precise moment I could not have cared less. I was about to play Shadow Creek.

I have played a few great golf courses in my day. And as I stood on the first tee of each of those world-class tracks, what I felt must have been something like what devout Catholics feel as they enter the Vatican, or what attractive young women feel when they enter George Clooney's house. It's a combination of respect, admiration, appreciation, and anticipation.

Looking out over the first fairway of Shadow Creek, I some-how felt tiny and enormous at the same time.

As I teed up my ball, Rick told me, "Remember. You've got to pace yourself out here too."

At first I thought he was trying to psych me out like the majority of people with whom I play golf. But then I realized that he was just trying to help. He could tell how jacked up I was. I had already started wondering where I should try to play this tee shot. And what I would do if I sprayed it right into the gorse, or yanked it left into the trees. Rick was right. I had to take it easy and pace myself.

I took a deep breath, stepped up to the ball, and striped it right down the middle.

I played out of my head that afternoon. I made crazy swirl-ing forty-foot putts. I blasted out of fairway bunkers to inches from the hole. I pounded a drive over three hundred yards on the signature fifteenth. And the whole time Rick and I talked about whatever: baseball, TV, politics, choriz. It was incred-ibly hot out but it didn't bother me. Instead of complaining, I allowed the sun's warmth to pour into my body and loosen up my joints. I felt myself turning farther on my backswing than I could ever remember. I felt easy and confident and peaceful. The more relaxed I became, the better results I had with my golf shots. I had always assumed that difficult shots required tremendous effort. But here I was firing at the pins like I was tossing horseshoes at a state fair.

At one point I thought that Rick had spiked the pitcher of Arnold Palmers with beta blockers. But he assured me that I was going low based purely on my talent and my attitude.

"You see, Bobby. If you want to have fun gambling, then you have fun gambling. And if gambling stops being fun, then you take a break and hit some golf balls. If you get tired of doing that, you shoot some pool or read a book. And pretty soon you'll be ready to start gambling again. When I say, 'pace yourself,' I mean, 'take it easy.' Don't beat yourself up, guy. There's too many people out there waiting to do that for you."

By the sixteenth hole I was in a state of bliss—what those yoga idiots always talk about but I could never achieve because even stretching to tie my shoes burns my hamstrings like hellfire. I finished up par, bogey, par to shoot an eighty-three from the tips of the most challenging and beautiful golf course I had ever laid eyes on.

By the time we got back to the clubhouse for a drink and a bite to eat, I was convinced that it made absolutely no difference if Rick was who he said he was or a total liar—I had met my guru.

I insisted on paying for the meal. Rick acquiesced but it turned out my adamant stand was wasted since the staff refused to accept payment. The maître d' passed along Mr. Wynn's best wishes. He was currently white-water rafting in South Africa but he hoped to see Rick soon. I figured if he could go white-water rafting, he could probably go heli-skiing too. So good news—Rick wasn't full of shit!

He asked me if I was feeling a little better after our round. I told him that I had never felt better. Then he asked me if I was ready to hit the casinos again and put a serious hurting on the house. I told him to lead the way.

20

That night we hit Vegas and hit it hard. From the Bellagio to Caesars to the Mirage to Treasure Island and then across the Strip to the Venetian, Harrah's, the Flamingo, the Paris, and Planet Hollywood, we went bananas. We played blackjack, roulette, Pai Gow poker, three-card poker, Caribbean stud, and Let It Ride. And we won everywhere. To this day I still don't know the rules to Caribbean stud, but I can tell you that I beat it for eight hundred dollars. Whenever the action started to turn against us, we'd cash in and head for the next table, the next game, or the next casino.

At the Venetian we played Spanish twenty-one at one hundred dollars a hand. I had no idea at the time what made it different from regular twenty-one—or, for that matter, what made it Spanish. The dealer, whose name was, somewhat boringly, Peter, dealt me two sevens of hearts. His up card was also a seven of hearts. When my second seven of hearts came up, Rick nudged me in the ribs and told me that this was the one.

Everyone else around the table started chattering and pointing at me. I had absolutely no idea what they were talking
about. All I knew was that I was looking at a fourteen against
a probable seventeen and I needed some help.

I told Peter to hit me. He wished me luck and then peeled
off a seven of hearts from the shoe. The place went insane. I
thought it was strange that everyone was so excited that I had
hit twenty-one. Lots of people hit twenty-one and no one
started hollering and applauding for them. Even the normally
unflappable Rick was jumping up and down and telling everyone to "Check out my boy!"

The pit boss clapped Peter on the back and told him to pay
me off. Then he congratulated me while the cheering and
screaming continued. The reason for all the excitement became clear to me when Peter reached into his chip well and
handed me five yellow chips. I was completely perplexed—
yellows are worth $1,000 each. Since when does twenty-one
pay fifty to one?

Rick explained to me that one of the bizarre rules of Spanish twenty-one is that if the player gets three suited sevens that
exactly match the dealer's seven it's called a "super bonus" and
he gets paid out to the tune of five G's. I was stunned. Then
it turned out that everyone else at the table received an "envy
bonus" just for playing with me when I hit the big one. So
they each got $50. The amount of enthusiasm and goodwill
was almost overwhelming. I had complete strangers getting me
drinks of every hue and flavor. Granted, the drinks weren't
costing anyone anything, but they were tipping the cocktail
waitresses extravagantly on my behalf.

For the next hour I was the hero of the Venetian. A family
of four visiting from Cameroon asked me to take a picture with
them in a gondola. Peter even asked me to take a picture with

him with the four sevens of hearts still on the table. Apparently he was getting some residual celebrity for having dealt that rarest of rare hands. He also got a healthy tip from yours truly.

Rick was pumped for me. Even he had never seen a super bonus, and he had spent more than his fair share of time in Vegas. He told me to enjoy the rush I was on. The winning wouldn't last forever. But, if I could hold on to that enormous, overpowering feeling of happiness and warmth, I could tap into it whenever I needed to. Rick didn't believe in "luck" in the traditional sense. He didn't think that some people were lucky while others were doomed to be unlucky. He just thought that it was important to recognize when good luck came your way and to really appreciate it. I could see what he meant. Being lucky is such a fickle concept. You grasp on to it during good times and then lament its absence when things go south. If you're too convinced that you've been bitten by good or bad luck, it prevents you from having the resolve to get the job done regardless of how your luck happens to be falling.

But if you just take those lucky moments for what they are—happy accidents raining down from the sky—then who gives a crap why they're happening or when they might come again? Just the other day I slammed my bare foot against the side of my bathtub. It stung so badly that my eyes started to tear up like when you yank out a clump of nose hairs all of a sudden (please tell me that this has happened to you too). I sat down on the edge of the tub and massaged my aching foot. It hurt like a bastard—but while I sat there, I suddenly remembered seeing that third seven of hearts land on top of its two identical triplet sisters. I don't know why that image popped up. I didn't summon it as a talisman to ward off toe pain. I just suddenly remembered it—and I smiled. That didn't stop my toe from hurting, but it definitely helped ease the pain.

I've been lucky and unlucky in my life, just like everyone. And, in the future, I'll be unlucky and lucky again. Rick just reminded me of that fact. And he encouraged me to hang on to the good moments, and let the crappy ones slide on by.

Rick told me that winning the super bonus was a sign. It was time to shift over to some sports betting. I had already accepted Rick as my personal lord and savior by this time, so I heeded his opinion on this matter. We cashed out our checks and headed back to the Bellagio.

21

The sports book at the Bellagio is what it would look like if Pete Rose's brain exploded inside the supercomputer that runs all the neon signs in downtown Tokyo. It's a fantasmagorical Venn diagram dedicated to the overlapping of sports, gambling, the Internet, television, and alcohol. Picture the biggest sports bar you've ever been in on Super Bowl Sunday. Now multiply that by one hundred, fill it with deranged action junkies, and fuel it with free booze. You have just created a pale approximation of a sleepy Tuesday morning at the Bellagio.

There is a fundamental difference between betting on sports and betting on table games. Regardless of what anyone tells you, luck is the common denominator of all table games. The rules are simple. The variations of how you can bet and what you can do once you have already bet are pretty limited. Ultimately, whether you win or lose comes down to luck. I don't care if you're married to the modified Kogen, or if you subscribe to any of the other hundred billion betting schemes out there. When you're playing blackjack, your fate depends upon the vagaries of the cards.

And I don't want to hear any nonsense about card counting. I read *Bringing Down the House* and I saw the movie *21*. Preposterous! All counting cards does is create a slight statistical advantage for the person (or persons) counting the cards. It's not a magic trick. Just 'cause you can count cards and have deciphered that there's an increased statistical probability that a ten will show up doesn't mean that a ten is definitely going to be the next card played. Card counting doesn't turn you into an all-powerful wizard. It just helps out a tiny bit.

Roulette—while thoroughly enjoyable, and my favorite metaphor for life itself—is so simple that a complete idiot can enjoy it (yet one more way in which it is like life). People actually talk about "roulette systems." That's stupider than the movie *21*. What system is going to predict where a ball will fall on a spinning wheel? Unless your system involves some kind of predictable shift in the earth's gravitational pull, you're just guessing along with the rest of us.

Craps has some math-based logic decisions that can help prevent betting against your own money, but even that doesn't require any skill or knowledge. Hey—can you throw two dice onto a table? Great! Then you can play craps. You want to know how easy it is to play craps? I have played craps before, and I have already gone on record saying that I have no idea how to play craps.

But sports betting is a whole other kettle of fish. The jury is still out on whether or not expert knowledge can actually improve your chances of winning when betting on sports. What is no longer up for debate, however, is that everyone who bets on sports is *positive* that their expert knowledge will improve their chances of winning.

Nobody bets twenty-nine on a roulette wheel and then gives you twenty reasons why twenty-nine is definitely going to hit. Well, I shouldn't say "nobody." Frankly, this is just the kind of thing that I would say to a table filled with goofballs and juice heads. But when I do it, it's just messing around. Stop by the sports book, however, and the guy with the Chief Wahoo hat will talk your ear off for an hour explaining to you how the Indians are a lock to cover the over against the Royals because the heart of their lineup is batting .600 against Kansas City's entire starting rotation.

This gentleman is so sure of the outcome of the game based on his perspicacity and assiduous attention to detail that he has wagered his next month's rent check on it. When the Royals win the game 1–0, and the score never gets anywhere near the over, you will see him talking some other poor schmuck's ear off, explaining why you should take the Browns and lay the field goal. Cleveland is unbeaten at home in the snow over the past decade. They're a stone-cold lock!

To his credit, Rick was not one of these wide-eyed action addicts who deluded himself into thinking he had all the answers. He had a lot of information at his disposal. But he tempered it with a healthy dose of realism. And the final component that made him such an effective gambler was his feel.

Usually "feel" is a term reserved to describe the indescribable, or to explain the inexplicable. The race car driver doesn't have the most powerful engine, but he's got a real feel for the track, and that's why he wins. The surgeon had never seen a tumor like that before. He couldn't rely on experience, so he felt his way through the procedure. What is that supposed to mean? Nothing, right? When we don't know how the driver won, or how the surgeon excised the growth, we chalk it up to feel.

Well, it doesn't mean nothing. Having hung out next to Rick for those four months in Vegas (and quite a bit since then), I can personally attest to the existence of feel. Just because we can't describe or explain it, doesn't mean it's not real.

I don't want to get all mumbo-jumbo on you here, but Rick had a way of sensing things that most other people can't sense. Here's an example.

That first night at the Bellagio there was a Yankees/Angels game on one of the dozens of TV screens so large you could have played a hockey game on its surface except that the skates would have scratched the glass. The Angels' ace, John Lackey, was pitching and the Angels were up 5–0. Rick suggested that we place a bet on the Yankees to win. This was ridiculous. The Angels have owned the Yankees for years. The Bronx Bombers were getting bombed by the Angels' best pitcher and the game was halfway over.

But Rick had a feeling. And it wasn't some goofy, new-age vibration that he was picking up out of the ether. He said, "The Angels are finishing a long road trip. Their concentration will start to dip. Xavier Nady's just getting comfortable in pinstripes. He's due for a big game. And Girardi's resting Robbie Cano, so he'll be fresh in the late innings." Even with that piercing insight, I still thought he was a little nuts making that wager. But I went along with it. And damned if the Yankees didn't storm back to take an 8–5 lead (with Nady driving in three of the runs).

I couldn't believe it. I told Rick that he was a freaking genius. Everyone around us who had been laughing when we placed the bet (and got eight-to-one odds on our money, thank you very much) suddenly looked at us like gambling gods.

Then, in the top of the eighth, Mark Teixeira hit a grand slam for the Angels. Just like that the Yankees were losing again, 9–8. It was a gut-wrenching moment for the team. Joe Girardi looked like someone had just kneed him in the solar plexus. Everyone at the sports book started laughing at us again. I could feel Girardi's pain, as I had the distinct sensation that Mark Teixeira's grand slam had ricocheted off the top of a passing 4 train, sailed across the continent, and landed right in the middle of my pants. Even Rick looked stunned.

"Holy shit!" he exclaimed. "Did I not see that coming."

Lesser men might have doubted Rick at that point. We hadn't risked too much money on the tickets—a few hundred each. But this unanticipated turn of events clearly was indicative of a man who had lost his feel. He made a preposterous bet, had gotten lucky enough to almost win, and then had been slapped back down by the inevitability of fate.

But I had seen Rick in action and I already knew better than to doubt his hunches. Sure enough, in the bottom of the eighth, the Angels started booting the ball all over the park. The Yankees took advantage of their miscues and their bats woke up (Nady and Cano had key hits). And just like that the Yankees went ahead and won the game 14–9.

We collected our winnings while those around us who had laughed, bowed, and then laughed again gave us one last bow as we walked away. It was more of a sarcastic "We're not worthy" salute than an actual bow, but I could tell they were impressed. I was impressed too. Rick was right on the money in his statistical analysis of the game. But he also had the indefinable ability to sense when things were going to change. What do I know? Maybe he really could pick up on subtle shifts in biometric readings or energy waves or auras. All I know is that he would rather drink battery acid than talk about biometrics, energy, or auras.

Rick's mission is clear. He just wants to play around and have some fun. He believes in being informed, and then setting the information aside so that it doesn't tie you up while you get a feel for the way things are going. That's a good way to navigate your way through a sports book—and through life.

22

Over the next couple of months, I fell into a very pleasant pattern. I'd gamble for a while. If I was up big and wanted to celebrate, I'd head off to explore one of Vegas's numerous, immaculately manicured golf courses. If my gambling spree went in the crapper and I needed to take a break, I'd head off to explore one of Vegas's numerous, immaculately manicured golf courses. It was a pretty great pattern.

When golf went well, I was happy and rested. When golf went poorly, I was a tiny bit less happy but still rested. I'd say that I'd hook up with Rick for about half of the gambling forays and for almost all of the trips around the track. He was off doing his own thing a lot too. His own thing consisted of acting as a personal trainer to some of the biggest celebrities to pass through town. He also claimed to be working on a novel, so he spent a lot of time at the library. Really. There are around fifteen extremely pleasant libraries in Vegas, and Rick went to them all. I visited him there a few times and was astounded to witness the normalcy of the library community. I assumed that they'd all be reading books about poker and chaos theory as it applies to gambling. But it was mostly school groups learning about American Indians and UNLV students researching term papers.

Aside from being an excellent golfer, a fearless gambler, an engaging storyteller, and, apparently, a great personal trainer, Rick is also the most well-read person I have ever met. I have always had a stack of books that I wish I could be reading, but I don't have time because I have to . . . whatever. I have to pick up my wife's dry cleaning. I have to wash my car. I have to clean out the rain gutters. Well, instead of doing all those things, Rick went ahead and read that stack of books. Looking back, I should have read my stack too. When you think about it, my wife dumped me, it always rained right after I washed the car, and the rain would have cleaned out the gutters anyway. Nowadays I try not to let that stack of unread books get too high.

The best thing about the pattern that I fell into was that I really was learning to pace myself. I didn't feel that desperate need to pump up the action every second of every day like I did when I first got to town. I realized that the real reason I came to Las Vegas was to play—not necessarily gamble, or hit golf balls—but to *play*. Ultimately, that's the most appealing thing about the city. The whole place is a temple to leisure. Some people might say that's a silly reason for a city to exist. But I disagree. Life has too many serious moments as it is. Every day we're faced with a dozen choices that tie us up in knots. Should I send my kids to public school? Or should I take a second job and send them to private school? Should I put my mother in a nursing home? Or should I invite her to live with me?

Those are big decisions that have to be made. They're important—and I'm not diminishing their significance. But in Vegas, my toughest choices were things like, "Should I play from the blue tees or the white tees?" "Should I hit the Hard Rock or Mandalay Bay first?" Those decisions are unimportant —but I'm also not diminishing their significance. Because not everything has to be such a big deal all the time. If you don't unwind and just veg out with a beer and a swim-up blackjack table now and then, you'll make yourself nuts. And if you're nuts, you'll make the wrong decisions about the big stuff. And that's how you end up with three kids in private school and your senile mother living in your basement.

One element of my Vegas routine that I particularly enjoyed was living up to my reputation as a big-stakes gambler. As it turned out, my friend who had the connections at Bellagio had indeed told the management there that I was a high roller from the East Coast. Thanks to my continued run of casino wins— due in no small part to Rick's guidance coupled with a stretch of truly good fortune—I was actually able to put quite a bit of money into play on a regular basis. I won enough to get rated as a high-limit player in all the casinos in town. I lost enough to make them feel like I was the kind of guy they all wanted around. And then I usually won enough back again to fund the whole enterprise and keep the circle of life rolling along.

Because of my slightly deceptive introduction to the casino world, and thanks to my consistent winning, I was quickly re- ceiving the VIP treatment at every casino I went to. Rick was already a known and welcome commodity everywhere in Vegas. Together we were like visiting royalty. Well, maybe royalty is a stretch. Let's say we were treated like visiting nobility who occasionally spend a week at the royal hunting lodge and could get the king on their cell phones if they really had to.

I received free massages at the Mirage, saw free shows at the Paris, and ate free buffets everywhere. The Vegas buffet is often scoffed at in popular culture. And I will acknowledge that the quality of food pales in comparison to the many fine restaurants one finds at all the best casinos. But there's nothing quite as satisfying as a quality buffet, completely overstuffed with a cornucopia of culinary options.

The buffet is Vegas in a microcosm. It's a truly ecumenical melting pot. When you're cruising the different food sections, you'll come across every class, race, religion, ethnicity, gender, sexual preference, and shoe size. One time I even saw Howie Mandel!

The casino floors are the same way. If you're at the sports book or the Pai Gow tables, you might be sitting next to a homeless guy or you might be sitting next to the pope. Okay, it's unlikely that the pope would be playing Pai Gow. But maybe you'd see him somewhere classier—like the baccarat table. My point is that all are welcome equally. Everyone gets pumped when they win and bummed when they lose. Everyone berates a dealer who's killing them, and laughs with a dealer who is treating them kindly.

Maybe I loved my time in Vegas so much because in a lot of ways it reminded me of the pubs of Ireland. There's a shared spirit in both places, a common and unique vocabulary that we all speak to each other while playing or drinking. Both cultures are built around activities that some people frown upon (drinking and gambling). And I realize that both can be abused and both can be harmful. But when approached the right way—the way I feel that I approached them during my time in Dublin and Vegas—then there's nothing more heartwarming and human than sharing a beer and a bet with fellow strangers.

23

I had an unbelievable time in that shimmering jewel set in the baking desert sands. The fact that at one point I was up over 100K is completely beside the point. Rick loved to talk about gambling, but he rarely talked about money. He really didn't care about it all that much. His attitude was that you worry about money only when you clearly don't have enough of it to do what you want. As long as his basic needs were met, he didn't sweat it. Obviously, a lot of his basic needs (and be-yond) were met for free because he has the most impressive list of friends and contacts that I've ever seen. Maybe Jay-Z has a more star-studded Rolodex, but I've never seen Jay-Z's Rolodex. I have, however, scrolled through Rick's address book—and it reads like a who's who of business, finance, politics, and the arts. I guess it pays to be a supremely person-able personal trainer.

As soon as I embraced Rick's laissez-faire approach to finance, my finances began to improve dramatically. That $100,000 number really is just an estimate because I stopped keeping track of my wins and losses. I knew that I was consistently up. And I knew that I would have to establish a rough tally of my profits by the end of the year—if only to give Uncle Sam his April rake. But the numbers weren't the goal. Having fun, getting my heart pumping by goosing the action, meeting new people, hitting golf shots I'd never tried before, seeing how long I could hold my breath underwater at the Palms rooftop pool—those became my new goals. The eight hundred dollars I won when I was able to hold my breath for over a minute was purely incidental. I think I blew it all buying everyone there shots anyway.

I was committed to searching out fun in all of its forms. The only thing that I consciously avoided doing while there was playing poker. I love poker. And I knew that I would love the poker scene in Vegas. My concern was that I would love it so much I would allow it to take over all my time. It's kind of like golf that way. If I could play golf twenty-four hours a day while being fed intravenously, I might spend the rest of my days smacking that pill around. But I can't play golf twenty-four hours a day. It's technically impossible, thank God. Poker, however, is extremely easy to play nonstop. And you don't even need the intravenous feeding tubes because they'll bring food right to your table (if the stakes are high enough).

Early on in my trip to Vegas I decided that I would save poker for the next time I checked out of my life in search of new thrills. And I wouldn't just play in Vegas. The poker scene has exploded to such a degree that I could follow the pro circuit around the globe all year long. Someday I'm going to take a stab at testing myself against the greatest players in the world. But that would have to wait for another time. For now, I was focusing on the simpler Vegas pleasures—table games, sports betting, and golf, with the occasional workout session with Rick thrown in just to keep my body from atrophying completely.

Just like in Ireland, when I stopped trying to force the fun, the fun came right to me all by itself. I had friends in every casino and clubhouse in town. I usually insisted upon interacting with the employees of the different establishments according to the theme of that establishment. Therefore, at the Paris, they called me Monsieur Sullivan. At the Venetian, they called me Roberto. At Treasure Island, I'd adopt a pirate's brogue and threaten to keelhaul the dealer if he didn't bust. It sounds kind of stupid, but we had a good time with it. The bottom line is—sure, people go to Vegas and hope to break the bank, but basically all they're really looking for is a good time. And, if you help them achieve their goals, they'll provide you with a good time too.

I had more amazing experiences there than I could possibly recount. But my ultimate twenty-four-hour stretch in Las Vegas occurred somewhere toward the end of my sojourn there—I think it was in late August.

I woke up really early, around 5 AM, because Rick and I were trying a new course and we wanted to get out there before it got to be so hot that my seven iron would melt in my hands. We got to the Royal Links Golf Club and they let us out before they were even open. Apparently Rick had helped Pete Dye lose thirty pounds and he was hooked up at all his golf courses. So we played the entire round without ever seeing another living soul.

Royal Links is the apotheosis of everything that's wonderful about Las Vegas. It's a completely preposterous concept—they re-created eighteen of the greatest links holes from England, Scotland, and Ireland and laid them out in succession in the middle of the Nevada desert. It sounds like a truly tacky, kitschy, Vegas-y idea. And it is. I mean, why would there be a links course in Las Vegas? Links courses occur naturally in blustery seaside conditions. There was nothing blustery or seaside-y about the sun-blasted heat flats of Nevada. But—like so many other tacky, kitschy ideas in Vegas—this one worked beautifully. The course was in perfect condition. The holes were breathtaking. And, let's face it, I had been in Ireland for four months and never dragged my ass out to a single links course. In one fell swoop in Vegas, I got to play eighteen of them.

Beyond the majesty of the surroundings, my game was on that morning. I don't know what happened exactly, because I've never been able to recapture that kind of swing magic since. Maybe I was just too tired from lack of sleep and too overwhelmed by the gorgeous scenery to worry too much about mechanics. But I was on fire from the first tee. As breaking eighty shifted from a remote possibility to a real chance, I didn't even tense up or get flustered. Rick was awesome. He kept me loose with a steady stream of humorous bullshit. As I stood at the eighteenth tee, I realized that I could par the hole for a seventy-nine. Instead of immediately regretting this realization as an inevitable jinx, I offered to bet Rick that I was breaking eighty today. Rick was up for the action.

He said, "You're on. One hundred bucks if you break eighty. But let's pump up the action. Let's add another one hundred dollars for each stroke over or under eighty. So, let's just say you were to yank this tee shot into the gorse and then take a quadruple here. You'd shoot an eighty-three and you'd owe me four hundred dollars—one hundred for not breaking eighty, and three hundred more because you'd be three over. What do you say?"

I didn't even hesitate. I told him that he was on. I believe my actual words were, "You're on, sucka."

I bombed a drive right down the middle. Crushed a three wood onto the green for my second. Just missed a curling forty-footer for eagle and tapped in for birdie. Seventy-eight! I couldn't believe it. It had been almost effortless. And the best part was that Rick was even happier for me than I was. I think he knew that his raising the stakes would help me buckle down and focus. He could tell that I was ready to rise to the occasion.

I gladly accepted his cash and told him I knew just what to do with it.

An hour later Rick, the pretty waitress from Prime, one of her equally pretty girlfriends, and I were in a helicopter heading out for a tour of the Grand Canyon. I will not waste your time or my meager brainpower trying to describe how insanely amazing the Grand Canyon is. All I can say is that swooping into the mouth of the canyon and descending all the way to land on the canyon floor is one of the most jaw-droppingly wonderful experiences that I have ever had. The four of us enjoyed a picnic lunch on the canyon floor while we stared all around us in stunned silence. The food was delicious, the ladies were lovely, and the setting was unbelievable in the truest sense of the word. Even though I was there looking right at it, I really had a hard time believing it was true.

The helicopter whisked us back to Vegas. We said good-bye to the girls. Even in my sexually disinterested emotional lethargy, I managed to make out briefly with the pretty waitress's pretty friend. Then Rick and I headed back to the Bellagio for an evening of debauched gambling.

As I got into the elevator to head up to my room to change, three middle-aged women entered behind me. I overheard them complaining about the convention for which they'd come to town. They were not pleased about it.

The tallest one of the three whose face kind of resembled a schnauzer said to her two friends (whose faces resembled other, slightly more attractive breeds), "What were they thinking, holding this convention in Las Vegas? Ugh—this place is the antithesis of spirituality."

Right there I threw up a little in my mouth. Apparently they owned a company that sold yoga DVDs or yoga clothes or something like that. They were meeting like-minded spiritual types to talk about growth and wholeness and finding your center. I'm sure they were also hoping to sell a whole lot of yoga DVDs or yoga clothes or whatever while they were there. All I know is that all three of them were carrying those little rolled-up yoga mats that the yoga people always tote around with them. But these yoga mats were made by Marc Jacobs— it said so right on the label! They probably cost a thousand dollars each. Overpriced, high-fashion yoga mats for snooty, self-obsessed yoga broads. And they were complaining that Las Vegas is the antithesis of spirituality.

Somehow the world's fastest elevator took forever that trip. Some little kid got on and pushed a thousand buttons. Then the three ladies couldn't remember which floor they were each on. The fates were trying hard to harsh my mellow—but I was too strong for them. My beatific day trumped their negativity and small-mindedness. I forced down my rising gorge and pleasantly bid them *adieu* as they left. Honestly. I actually said to them, "*Adieu*, ladies!" At least I got a chuckle out of it.

After I'd showered and changed, I met Rick down in the sports book to implement a bold new plan that we had been talking about recently. Our sassy idea was for one night to bet only trifectas. And we weren't just talking about horse racing.

We decided to maximize our potential profits through the roof by bunching all of our bets into conjoined threesomes. We weren't just going to pick the Yankees to win, for example. We'd parlay that Yankee win with a Dodger win and a Cubs win. It would be one bet with three outcomes. If any of the teams didn't win, then the whole bet was off. But if all three teams won, then the three-way bet paid off at an exorbitant rate.

Rick and I pooled our accumulated information. Then we pooled our accumulated sense of feel. In truth, he added a lot more to both pools. But, by this point, I had become pretty adept at getting the info, and then not letting it get in my way. I had a vibe on some games. And I picked two horse-racing trifectas that I felt good about too. We were stomping around the sports book talking to the regulars and telling everyone who would listen about our bold new scheme. Some of them made fun of us. Some of them jumped on our action. One of them bought us a round of drinks. Then I returned the favor. Everyone was in a good mood.

As we settled down to watch the mind-numbing multitude of events that were happening simultaneously on the myriad big screens, I felt completely content. I didn't even care if I won or lost the bets because it was so clear to me that I had already won. In one day I had already shot the low round of my life on a beautiful golf course, I had witnessed one of the most stunning sights on the planet, I had kissed a hot Vegas hoochie, and now I was throwing back shots of Bushmills while a thousand games flashed before my eyes. It had turned out to be a pretty great day.

The pretty great day turned into an absolutely great night because we won almost every trifecta we played. It was crazy. And it wasn't because we were so smart or our feel was so powerful. We just stumbled into one of those runs of good luck that has to be experienced to be appreciated. And, believe me, we appreciated the hell out of it. Maybe we laid out a total of two thousand dollars in initial wagers. By the time the evening was almost over, we must have taken in around fifty thousand dollars. We were heroes at the sports book. At one point some visiting frat brothers from Ohio State who had piggybacked a winning trifecta I picked at Saratoga actually lifted me onto their shoulders and carried me around the room.

Our last wager of the night was our biggest one yet—we had invested our whole trifecta-derived bankroll into one superparlay. We were betting three different events in three different continents in three different sports (American harness racing, Japanese professional soccer, and Australian-rules football). The atmosphere in the room was electric as we won the first two propositions. The crowd was behind us, cheering us on to break the bank. We didn't even know the rules to Australian-rules football, and we still had a blast watching the action beamed across the planet to the Bellagio's satellite receptors. Everything was on the line in the final game, and we were about to win. But at the last second, a botched torpedo punt resulted in the visiting team scoring a behind (whatever the hell all that was supposed to mean) and we lost the whole damned bet. All of the night's winnings were wiped out in a single blow.

The crowd was stunned. They thought we'd go berserk. We'd been so close to some serious cash, only to see it all evaporate. We had just lost everything—the brutal nut punch that all gamblers dread. It was time to start hurling chairs and cold-cocking pit bosses. But Rick and I looked at each other and just started laughing. We were both thinking the same thing—Vegas math. Sure, we just blew around fifty thousand bucks. But in sheer Vegas math numbers we were still up huge for the day. I'd say that in terms of raw fun-to-dollars, I was ahead at least a quarter million bones.

The sports book closed, but the party didn't stop. We all moved to the tables. I was running around making crazy bets with the few chips I had left. I won some, lost some—who knows what happened exactly? I know I did many flaming Apple Passion shots, and I think I did a handstand in between the dancing fountains. By three in the morning, I was so tired and drunk and exhilarated that I could barely walk. I said good night to everyone—about half of them insisted on hugging me—and headed for my room.

I dragged myself into my suite and collapsed on my bed. I hadn't closed the Super Shades so the lights of the Strip filled my room. At three in the morning it looked like the universe had been flipped upside down. The sky was black but the ground was full of stars. I could have pressed the button by my bedside that automatically closed the shades, but I decided to sleep with them open. Let the stars shine, I thought. Life is good.

24

Just like in Ireland, I somehow sensed that the end of my stay was close at hand. I wasn't being kicked out of my hotel room or anything. And I still didn't have any firm plans for what I'd do next. But I could just tell that it was time to move on. I began to contemplate the next phase of my adventure. I had drunk my fill in Ireland. Now I was playing like a blissful, conscienceless reprobate in Vegas. What should I do now? What was I missing?

For some reason, my first thought was Alicia. But why would I be missing a documentary filmmaker I'd met only once—even if she was extremely cute, funny, and charismatic? I pushed her out of my mind—no point in obsessing over missed opportunities. I forged ahead with my checklist of things I needed to accomplish.

I still didn't know how to drive a stick shift, but I had really stopped caring about that by now. Rick had taught me how to play craps, and I was enjoying that greatly. I especially liked pressing all the Hard Ways, playing the Hi-Lo, and hitting a $20 Yo. Seriously, the craps vocabulary is one of the greatest inventions in the history of the universe. Every time I roll the bones now I feel like I'm in a Damon Runyon short story. I may look into changing my name to Nicely-Nicely.

But I knew there was still something missing—something that needed to be addressed in the remaining four months of my yearlong extravaganza. And then the answer leapt out at me. I suddenly realized that what was missing was sex. Maybe not just sex, but intimacy, tenderness—you know—*girls*. I was just about through with this extended bout of celibacy first caused by my wife's lack of affection, then by her lack of not having sex with someone named David, then by the emotional coma she had left me in.

It's hard for people to believe but I really just hadn't been that interested in sex during my time away. Sure there was a drunken flirtation with Giovanna and a bunch of other sexy, boozed-up floozies in the bars of Ireland. Then there was my mini make-out session with the Grand Canyon girl. And Lord knows that Vegas is filled with stunning women who miraculously appear every time you hit it big at the tables. But I just never had that overwhelming urge to do anything about it. Of course when I was on my own I did something about it from time to time. But that's a private matter that will never be referred to again. The larger issue is that whatever the hell had gone wrong with my wife had left me romantically shell-shocked. Aside from my afternoon with Alicia, I could barely remember a single significant potentially romantic interaction that I'd had with a woman in the past seven months. Jesus— had it really been seven months already?

I took it as a good and healthy sign that I was starting to give serious thought to breaking that ugly streak. But how, where, when, and with whom should I go streak breaking? I decided to ask Rick's advice. If you can't get an opinion on sex from your personal guru, then what good is he?

True to form, Rick had many opinions on sex. His primary opinion was that he liked it. Rick had not been in an emotional coma while in Vegas. Frankly, I'm surprised that he wasn't in a coma-coma while in Vegas because the dude was banging constantly. But he was never sleazy or hypocritical about it. If he met a nice lady and they hit if off, one thing would lead to another. Sometimes they hung out for a while. Sometimes it was just a one night thing. But they were both just having fun and enjoying each other. I could sense that he respected my lack of involvement in this arena. He knew that when the time was right, I'd be ready. I told him that I was ready.

"It's about fucking time! I was worried you were turning into a eunuch."

Perhaps respect was too strong a word. Still, he didn't bust my balls about it; he just had some sound advice.

"Okay, first things first—do not ever go to a hooker."

I assured him that I was not about to go to a hooker. That was something I never had even the most remote interest in pursuing.

"Good. So number one is you're not going to any hookers. Number two is, you're going to Thailand."

I was confused. This seemed to be contradictory advice. If he didn't want me seeing any hookers, then why was he suggesting I visit the universal epicenter for prostitution?

"Bobby, have I ever steered you wrong?"

I was tempted to mention the time that he accidentally drove our golf cart into a drainage ditch, but I refrained. For the most part, his guidance was so helpful that I wondered why he hadn't recorded a self-help DVD. I told him as much.

"Thanks, man. So here's the deal. What you need isn't just sex. What you need is to wallow in pleasure for a change—pure, physical pleasure. This Vegas thing has been about fun and risk and play—and that's great. But you've spent your whole life doing the right thing, being the responsible one, taking care of everyone else. Now it's your turn to just lie back and soak up the things that make us human beings feel the best. I'm talking about sunshine, warm ocean water, soft sandy beaches, hammocks swaying in the breeze, morning dew glistening on a bowl of fresh-cut papaya. And yeah, I'm talking about sex—but only if the situation leads there naturally, romantically."

I pointed out that it sounded like he was talking about sending me to Fantasy Island.

"I am. Only it's not an island. It's an isthmus."

"Fantasy Isthmus?" I wondered aloud.

"No, Bobby. *Krabi* isthmus on the west coast of Thailand."

And that was that. I didn't need any more information or analysis. Rick said I should go to the Krabi isthmus on the west coast of Thailand, and I decided to go to Krabi isthmus on the west coast of Thailand. It sounded right. It felt right. Would I get laid there? Would I find love there? Would I get kidnapped by drug traffickers and forced to work as a heroin mule? Only time would tell. But I was ready and eager to find out.

Book Three
Thailand

or

"There is no remedy for love but to love more."
—Henry David Thoreau

or

12 Tales About Chasing Tail

25

Rick has spent quite a bit of time in the Far East over the years. Rick has spent quite a bit of time pretty much everywhere. Apparently, if you're a good enough personal trainer, word gets out there and wealthy people who are eager to get into shape will fly you around the globe to whack their glutes. Rick shared a great deal of his knowledge of Thailand—and Krabi in particular—with me. But we didn't have a lot of time before I left, so my education was incomplete. If you plan on traveling to Thailand there are many things that you should know, things Rick never got around to filling me in on. I will tell you some of these things—even though I had to learn them the hard way.

1) If you're in Las Vegas, and you suddenly get the over-whelming desire to visit the Krabi isthmus, prepare your-self for an insanely long trip. I had to fly from Vegas to LA, from LA to Taipei, from Taipei to Bangkok, from

Bangkok to Phuket, and finally I hopped on the ferry from Phuket to Krabi. All in all, it took me infinity hours. And that's not even factoring in the time change.

2) Just because you've been in a hot place like Las Vegas for four months, that doesn't mean you know squat about hot. Thailand is hot. Thailand is really hot. Thailand is like Vegas if there was a gigantic radiator just outside of Vegas leaking steamy-hot jungle vapor all over town all the time forever. And the air-conditioning is either terrible or nonexistent. That said, after a day or two of the intense moist warmth, it penetrated my whole system and I actually started to like it. That tropical vibe seeped into my soul. I felt like Fletcher Christian when he and the crew of the *Bounty* spent all that time in Tahiti and everybody "went native." (For the record, I like to think of myself as the Marlon Brando Fletcher Christian, not the Mel Gibson version.)

3) If someone wais you, wai them back. For the uninitiated out there, in Thailand the traditional form of unspoken greeting isn't a wave, or a wink, or a handshake, or a high five—it's the wai. That's where you put your palms together in front of your chest and bow your head in deference to the person whom you're greeting. I'll never forget the first time I got wai-ed. I had just gotten off the plane from Vegas in Suvarnabhumi Airport in Bangkok. (Suvarnabhumi is an extremely oddly named airport, but it still runs a distant second to Dublin's Aerfort Bhaile Átha Cliath.) As I approached a young man at the information counter, he gently placed his hands together and bowed his head. It looked like something straight out of a Bruce Lee movie. I swear to God, I thought he

was goofing with me. Perhaps I was overcome with jet lag and addled by fatigue but I actually made a gong sound and asked to see his Shaolin master. After explaining that kung fu was Chinese not Thai, the young man went on to inform me that in Thailand the wai is a respectful greeting. Not to return a wai is disrespectful. To respond to a wai with racist humor goes beyond disrespectful—it's a good way to get your ass kicked. I apologized profusely and asked for directions to my connecting flight. To his credit, the young man gave me those directions and chose not to kick my ass.

4) While we're on the subject of racism, I have another comment to make that might sound racist but really isn't: Asians do not like to wait on line. At least the Asians with whom I interacted didn't. I first discovered this as I crossed the tarmac to board the flight from Bangkok to Phuket, but this observation was later corroborated at every possible instance where line waiting would normally have been called for. In my four months in Thailand, no one ever waited in line voluntarily. As everyone left the main airport terminal, the narrow doorway created a natural and orderly single file. But as soon as we were outside, there was a mad swarm to reach the bottom of the movable staircase that led up to the plane. The throng was in such a rush to push forward to get on the plane faster that it ended up taking around five times longer to get everyone on the plane than it would have if we'd just kept that single file going. The disorganized melee didn't upset anyone. No one started yelling or throwing fists like they would have in America if chaos like that broke out. They just had absolutely no intention

of waiting in line. In fact, the only people who had any interest in maintaining the line were me and another American guy named Peter.

While Peter and I hung back and let the lunacy sort itself out, we got to talking. Peter was originally from Iowa but had moved to Los Angeles after college. He was going to go to graduate school, but couldn't get in, and couldn't have afforded it even if he had gotten in. Then he decided to be an actor, but he was terrible and couldn't get any work. He found himself in a strange town with no money, no connections, no plan for the future, and no marketable skills. So he became a writer. As he explains it, he had so little confidence in his ability to actually write anything that anyone would ever want to read that he decided to write TV sitcoms. And, since he had killed off most of his brain cells smoking pot and drinking beer, and had absolutely no interest in literature, art, or culture of any kind, he became an incredibly successful sitcom writer.

Peter actually created two hugely popular TV comedies that I can't name here for fear of being sued. As he tells it, he got fired from each hit show. Unlike in the real world, getting fired in Hollywood is, apparently, a wonderful thing. They paid him massive sums of money to go away, and then whoever took over made the shows even more successful. Since he created the shows and owned a big piece of them, he was the one who made the most money when they were sold into syndication. In essence, he got two huge paydays without really having to do any of the hard work.

In the happy aftermath of his great good fortune, Peter set his sights on more philanthropic pursuits. At least that's how he sees it. In my mind, buying breast implants for attractive would-be starlets, visiting the Playboy Mansion fortnightly, and traveling the world looking for the next ball-jangling hedonistic experience aren't exactly acts of philanthropy. But what do I know? If Andrew Carnegie had created *How I Met Your Mother,* he might have done the same thing. (Note: *How I Met Your Mother* is just an example. Peter *did not* create *How I Met Your Mother.*)

When I told Peter my story, he was extremely interested. Actually, at first he was extremely bored. Then he asked me for an abbreviated version of my story as he didn't think he had the patience to wait out the normal-length one. So I crystallized the nuggets for him—heartbreak, divorce, Ireland, Vegas, Krabi. That's when he got interested.

"This Rick guy was right on the money. If you're looking to get back on the horse—sexually speaking—then Thailand is definitely the place for you."

I'm not sure that "getting back on the sex horse" was exactly what I was aiming for, but I nodded politely. Peter was an interesting guy. And he was funny. And he spoke English, which was a huge plus. Frankly, it was nice to have someone to talk to while I killed time waiting for the jam-packed fish ball of Asian line-cutting humanity to squeeze itself up the stairs and into the airplane.

He was going to be staying at some fancy beachfront villa in Phuket and he suggested that we stay in touch. We exchanged information. Then he told me which Hollywood stars who are rumored to be gay really are gay, and which are not—and vice versa. I have since discovered that this is a popular topic of conversation in Hollywood. And I have to admit—it was pretty entertaining.

Peter and I parted ways at Phuket and I continued my endless trek on to Krabi. I have never been that good at math so I honestly cannot compute how many hours it took me to get to the hotel at Krabi. It was, without a doubt, the longest, most uncomfortable, most exhausting and unpleasant trip of my life. Upon entering the grounds of the hotel, however, I knew in an instant that every second was worth it. Rick was right yet again. The place was freaking paradise.

26

First things first: I will not tell you the name of the hotel. To even call it a hotel is to do it a disservice. Hotel sounds so pedestrian, so run-of-the-mill. And you can't just call up and make a reservation there anyway. So, technically, I guess it really isn't a hotel at all. It's kind of like that famous old Italian restaurant Rao's in New York City. You can't make a reservation to eat there—you have to already have one. But how can you already have one if you can't make one to begin with? I have no idea, but the joint is always packed. The only way to get in is to be invited by someone who has managed to circumvent the system by miraculously already having a reservation. My idyllic beachfront spot in Thailand operated under the same set of bizarre restrictions. Fortunately, I was friends with an insider.

Rick was my conduit to Eden. And I can't reveal the name and exact whereabouts of this tropical heaven on earth because I promised Rick I wouldn't. If I tell you, then you'll tell someone else, who'll tell his cousin, and she might mention it to her dentist—and before you know it there would be dentists there. And that would be unacceptable. There shouldn't be any dentists in paradise, right?

For the purpose of simplicity, I will call the spot where I spent most of my time while in Thailand the Cove. I will call it the Cove for two reasons. 1) The Cove sounds cool. And 2) It's in a cove.

Did anybody ever see that Leonardo DiCaprio movie *The Beach*? My wife tried to get me to go when it first came out, but I had absolutely no interest in seeing it. I remember thinking at the time that I'd rather go jogging than voluntarily see that piece of garbage—and I hate jogging. After I got back from Thailand, though, I went out and rented it. Guess what? It's even worse than I imagined. Beyond moronic—one of those movies that you forget about while you're watching it. Of course the beach itself is lovely. Soft white sand, warm turquoise water, dense, lush tropical foliage swaying in the breeze, natural plunge pools, brightly colored fish, and coral arches framing the setting sun. The scenery in that movie was truly stunning. But compared to the Cove, DiCaprio's beach looked like a greasy February morning on Coney Island after a circus freak convention and a cheap beer festival coincided with a condom giveaway.

It's hard to describe beauty. Ugly is pretty easy. I can describe something really vile (like that Coney Island image) and have you try and picture its diametrical opposite. But true beauty has to be experienced to be comprehended. When I hopped off the ferry in Krabi, I thought the setting was amazing. As Chula, the representative from the Cove who met me at the dock, drove me through some light underbrush in an open-top 4x4, I couldn't believe how much more striking the scenery was becoming. After we parked the 4x4, I was led onto a flat-bottomed skiff that was poled across a shallow tidal estuary. That was even more striking. And when we passed through an opening in the trees on the other side of the estuary, and bounced along a path through the jungle in another open-top Jeep, and I got my first glimpse of the Cove, I just sat there in shock. What I was looking at was so much more impressive than what I'd already been impressed by that I really could not process what I was seeing. The colors were more vibrant, the light seemed clearer, the smell in the air was unlike anything I'd ever experienced. The whole place just seemed more . . . *alive* than anywhere I had ever been. I feel like an idiot, but I just can't make these words tell you what I wish you could know. The Cove is beautiful. You'll just have to take my word for it and substitute in your mind's eye whatever beauty means to you.

Chula, God bless his heart, had obviously seen this kind of reaction many times before. He waited patiently for my paralysis to fade away. After a while he looked at me with a grin. "Nice, right?"

I looked down at him—he couldn't have been more than five feet tall—and nodded my head foolishly.

"Come," he said. "This is not even the nicest view. Just wait until you see your room!"

Chula lead me along a path toward a large teak structure that jutted out from the greenery. Exotic birds squawked and screeched in the air. Fluorescent geckos scrambled through the grass. I could only assume that adorable monkeys were eating ripe papayas in the treetops. As we approached the main hall, two of the most stunningly gorgeous coffee-colored women in brightly colored sarongs and bikini tops came down the steps and headed into the forest. There was a moment there that I literally thought my head might explode. I actually staggered briefly and had to reach out to the railing by the stairs to keep my feet underneath me. Chula patted me lightly on the back.

"It is a special place here, is it not? But your friend Rick sent a message for you that he asked me to relay. He says, 'Pace yourself, Bobby.'"

I laughed and shook the cobwebs out of my head. The transcontinental advice was just what I needed. I let go of the rail feeling sturdy again. Damn, that Rick is a good guru.

"Thanks, Chula. Lead on, my man."

27

I think I need to talk a little about sex now. Sex was the primary catalytic force behind my move to Thailand. Although, in my defense, it wasn't like I was some horny loser desperate to get laid. I just realized that a big part of my life that had been dormant for a long time was starting to wake up. Rick thought that the Cove would provide a soothing, pleasant wake-up call, as opposed to some other place that would be more like a harsh, buzzing alarm clock (Detroit, for example). Rick had been clear about why he was sending me here: I needed to soak up some serious physical pleasure, in all its forms. And he was right. It was like I had just finished a grueling, yearlong workout and all these muscles that I didn't even know I had before were suddenly aching from lack of use. I was finally ready to feel good. This was not about sex. This was about getting my body right along with my mind. But let's call it like it is: there's no way to talk about Thailand without dealing with the whole sex issue.

So here's the deal to the best of my limited understanding of the deal: prostitution is illegal in Thailand. It has been for over forty years. However, there's an interesting loophole in Thai law that says that, while prostitution is illegal, it's not illegal for establishments dedicated to legal pursuits to offer "special services." This means that you can't open up a whorehouse in Bangkok. You can, however, open up a massage parlor, or go-go bar, or pool hall, or tool-and-die factory and have the women working there offer up "special services" in exchange for a fee.

I am not being hyperbolic when I say that prostitution is everywhere in Thailand. My first week at the Cove, I borrowed a bicycle and rode the fifteen minutes into town to see what it was like. My first impression was that it was a charming but quiet seaside village—nothing out of the ordinary.

I entered a bookstore in the vain hope that they might have a *USA Today* (football season had begun). Unfortunately, the bookstore seemed to stock nothing but Buddhist texts. As a courtesy, I was doing a little browsing when a young woman who worked at the store wai-ed me politely. Having learned my lesson at the airport, I immediately wai-ed her back. Then the owner of the store asked me if I wanted to take this young woman into the back room for "relaxation." At first I was so flummoxed that I had no idea what he was talking about. I figured it out though when he told me that she would cost extra because she was "very, very virgin."

My initial reaction was to punch the guy in the face. I don't know why this was the case, but it was. The first emotion I felt was anger—as if this man had insulted me. My next reaction was to try and rescue this poor girl. I had to do something to protect this sweet, innocent who was being preyed upon by the Thai religious bookstore's version of Jabba the

Hutt. Upon further investigation, however, it turned out that the "virgin" was the owner's wife. She then acknowledged that she was only a "semivirgin" and I could have the relaxation at a discounted rate. The pair of them continued their one-sided negotiation with me as I got the hell out of there as fast as I could.

Obviously there are many men who would be delighted by the prospects of an unanticipated sexual liaison popping up while they were thumbing through a worn copy of *The Questions of King Milinda*. I am not one of those men. It actually grossed me out. Maybe it was the fact that all those Buddhist texts made me think of my ex-wife and I was in a weird, vulnerable, melancholy state when the hooker first approached me. I'm sure that my upbringing had more to do with my negative reaction than anything else. On a fantasy level, hooking up with a nameless stranger for a no-strings-attached encounter has its appeal. But there's something lodged deeply in my heart or brain or soul (or maybe all three) that completely prevented me from getting turned on by the reality of prostitution when it stared me in the face. I'm sure that narcissism has a lot to do with it too. I'd like to think that whatever woman I'm with wants me for me—not just my wallet. Which probably explains why I hadn't been with a woman in a long time.

But there are plenty of those other types of men in Thailand. As I left the bookstore, the semivirgin was heading into the back room with a fat, bearded white guy who must have been in his sixties and was definitely not there to further his religious education.

It wasn't like sex was being offered at every bookstore, tobacco shop, car dealership, and truck stop in Thailand. I mean, the place also functions totally normally like a million other places with kids going to school and grandmothers sweeping the front stoop. But over time it became apparent that, on some level, sex had crept deeply into the fabric of Thai society. It would clearly be very difficult to separate sex from mainstream Thai life, in part because of the popular perception of the country as a cauldron of carnality.

The following is a snippet of an actual conversation that I overheard on the street, in front of the bookstore, as I was leaving. Two young guys with thick Cockney accents were engaged in a heated debate. One of them was heading into the bookstore and his friend had stopped him.

Brit. #1: "Oi, what the fuck you wanna go 'ere for? I want to get fucked not read a bloody book!"

Brit. #2: "They fuck you 'ere, you stupid cunt. They fuck you everywhere in this fucking country!"

Whether or not the second gentleman's observation is factually accurate is almost beside the point. He believed it. Many other people believe it. So does the demand meet the supply or does the supply meet the demand? What difference does it make? All I know is that Thailand is a truly stunning country with warm people, a rich cultural history, and delicious food—but when you say "Bangkok," all anybody thinks of is go-go bars and donkey shows.

I know absolutely nothing about go-go bars and donkey shows. I don't even know if donkey shows are real or just some bullshit story I once heard involving Bette Davis and Tijuana. If you want to read about the seedy underbelly of the Thai sex scene, don't come to me. I got freaked out when some chick in a bookstore wanted to blow me for a few baht. I had absolutely no interest in going any deeper into the lion's den. Just walking past some of the hard-core bars and massage parlors made me really uneasy. Seeing the crowds of guys window shopping for sad young women with huge fake smiles actually made me queasy.

But I'm no moral crusader. I understand that there's a complex social and economic dynamic going on behind all that leering and paying and thrusting and poking. If I'd ever seen any children in jeopardy I would have gone completely nuts and tried to do something about it. If I'd ever witnessed a woman being forced to do something against her will, I would have tried to protect her. But I didn't. What consenting men and women (in any combination thereof) do together in exchange for cash is entirely their business. In my limited exposure to that whole world I just saw a bunch of adults of (in my opinion) questionable character and/or happiness engaged in a sexual and political tug-of-war as old as time. In the final analysis, my take on prostitution in Thailand is: to each his (or her) own. So I didn't want to buy sex in a Buddhist bookstore. Big deal. I didn't want to buy any Buddhist books there either.

I wasn't in Thailand to get laid. I was in Thailand to feel good. And nowhere on earth made me feel as good as I felt when I was at the Cove. So, for the most part, that's where I spent my time. When you've been handed the keys to paradise, it would be foolish to waste a lot of time outside the gates.

28

I will now cut directly to the chase: during my second week at the Cove . . . I got laid. I realize that it is extremely ungentlemanly to make that statement, and I apologize to anyone who may have been rooting for me to turn out to be a gentleman. I do my best—and I have been known occasionally to rise in the presence of a lady and hold a door or two open for the elderly —but this book does have the word "fuck" in the title, and I have certain responsibilities to my readership.

Here's how it happened—and I'll try to keep things as polite as possible. I'll also try to keep things as accurate as possible since I'm a little fuzzy on some of the details for reasons that you will soon discover.

As I've already mentioned, the Cove is not like a traditional hotel in many ways. First of all, it's located in the Garden of Eden, if the Garden of Eden had been located directly on the shores of the most gorgeous tropical lagoon in the solar system. Secondly, the clientele were not your run-of-the-mill tourists. The only people who knew about the Cove and who had any access to it were individuals of great standing in the worlds of art, fashion, literature, finance, technology, politics, entertainment, sports, science, and—apparently—personal training. The place housed a rotating assortment of nothing but the best, the smartest, the most accomplished, and the most beautiful. I felt like a worthless schlub there compared to all these shining specimens of human achievement. And I'm sure that, if most of them had gotten to know me, they would have felt the same way. Thirdly, the main structure at the Cove was a central reception area that housed only a restaurant and the registration and concierge desks. The rest of the buildings were gloriously appointed individual bungalows perched directly on the beach, with ample patios cantilevered out over the water. Each bungalow felt completely secluded from the others due to the naturally occurring ribbonlike perimeter of the shoreline. Small pockets of fine white-sand beach were separated from one another by lush, sweet-smelling clumps of jungle. So when you were in your room—or I should say rooms, because all of the bungalows were like small, tasteful mansions —you felt that you were the only person in the world. This wasn't a hotel, it was a heavenly oasis of solitude, beauty, and calm.

You can imagine my surprise then when I was suddenly woken up at six in the morning on the Tuesday of my second week in Thailand by a stereo blasting Akon's "Smack That Ass" at full volume (I believe that Eminem also makes a cameo appearance on the track). Even stranger and more annoying than the loud, horrible music was that I couldn't figure out where the hell it was coming from. It sounded like the source was the bungalow itself. I'd heard of people's braces picking up radio frequencies but, to my knowledge, this phenomenon has never been attributed to mahogany floorboards, muslin window treatments, or delicately carved teak bedposts.

I finally tracked down the source of the "Ass Smacking" to my patio. Upon further analysis, I realized that the tunes were actually coming from underneath my patio. I lay down on my stomach, shoved my body out over the cantilevered deck, and looked—upside down—underneath. There, in the shade of my deck, bobbing up and down on the gentle surf that lapped against the shore, was the flat-bottomed skiff that the Cove used to transport guests to and from town. Inside the skiff was a large, '70s-style boom box blasting the Akon song. And next to the boom box was an attractive young Indian woman wearing a lime green bikini and a tropical print sarong. She was either deeply asleep, profoundly unconscious, or utterly dead.

It turned out that option two was closest to the truth. Her name was Devika and she was on vacation at the Cove with her mother and father, who was the Indian ambassador to Japan. She had swiped one of the skiffs, headed into town last night, and gotten epically hammered. When she was heading back to the Cove she decided to do some last-minute tequila shots while jamming out to the radio. She passed out and ended up floating underneath my bungalow.

She was also very cute—at least she was the cutest girl who ever washed up under my porch before. She was a bit on the plump side, with smooth brown skin, long black hair tied up in a braid, and a body so delightfully curvaceous that upon glancing at it, you immediately wanted to ride it like a roller coaster. At least I did.

Once she regained consciousness, she wouldn't stop talking. She was eager to tell me all about herself and her fascinating life in Japan where she spent most of her time shopping, playing pachinko for money, and drinking copious amounts of sake.

She seemed to have absolutely no interest in who I was or why I was at the Cove. And I must admit that there was something appealing about this lack of curiosity. For some reason she seemed to enjoy my company and instantly made plans for us to go snorkeling and then have lunch. I could not come up with a single reason to say no, so I said yes and threw on a bathing suit. Forty-five minutes later we were checking out clown fish and conger eels and spiny lobsters. An hour later we were eating pad thai and sautéed monk fish on my patio. We were also doing many shots of Thai scorpion vodka.

Thai scorpion vodka turns out to be vodka with a scorpion in it. Yup. A scorpion. Legend has it that the scorpion has aphrodisiacal qualities. All I know is that the vodka has drunk qualities. Maybe I thought I was in better "drinking shape" after my time in Ireland, but those shots out on the patio in the brilliant tropical sun demolished me. Devika also seemed well on her way to a repeat performance of her previous evening's escapades.

Around five minutes after the vodka ran out, Devika and I had somehow staggered to my bedroom, managed to clamber onto the bed, and—even more surprisingly—figured out a way to stay conscious long enough to have sex.

29

Vodka is an extremely powerful liquid. Scorpions are lethally venomous insects. It stands to reason that when you combine the two, craziness is sure to ensue. And ensue it did. I was plastered enough to not really remember all the details of that first intertwining with a great deal of accuracy. But I wasn't so plastered that I couldn't handle my business. After an extended hiatus from the horizontal mambo, I was a little bit rusty but eager to show off my floor moves. And Devika was an ideal dance partner.

Okay, the dance analogy is getting a little clunky but I'm just not comfortable sharing the intimate details of my sex life without buffering them with metaphor. Let's just say that what I remember of that intial encounter was pretty awesome. Devika was eager, sexy, and limber as hell. And if I didn't exactly set her world on fire, I'm pretty sure that I acquitted myself respectably. Why she had picked me was a mystery that I had no interest in solving. We fit together well and were having fun. Only a total fool would mess with that kind of serendipity. And, fortunately, I'm not a *total* fool.

For the next few weeks, I developed an extremely pleasant routine at the Cove. I'd wake up early with the sun, the squawking macaws, and the jabbering monkeys. Usually I'd be slightly hungover. Usually Devika would be sound asleep on, next to, or beneath my bed. Her parents had taken an extended side trip to Cambodia, so their presence wasn't an issue (thank God). I'm not sure I would have had the stones to keep sleeping with the daughter if, in between trysts, I'd had to engage the father in lengthy discussions about cricket and the thorny problems in Kashmir.

After I woke up, I'd throw on a bathing suit, jump off the porch into the bay, and swim along the shoreline toward the main building. Then I'd scarf down a sensible breakfast of fresh-cut papaya and a large glass of mango juice. Then I'd jog back along the beach to my bungalow.

A quick aside about food in Thailand. First of all, it is, in my opinion, delicious. I love the combination of sweet and savory—things like chicken stewed in coconut milk and shrimp sautéed alongside pineapple. Their breakfasts, however, are a cause for concern. Seeing as how I was in Thailand to reconnect with raw, basic physical pleasures, I stuck with the fresh fruit. But most Thais breakfast on a variety of thick porridges filled with rice, egg, and pork. Another popular breakfast dish features pig heart, liver, kidneys, and intestines (plus some leafy green vegetables thrown in for good measure). I have tasted many of these traditional dishes and they're actually not bad. I just couldn't start the day with them. I'm a child of Frosted Flakes and OJ—not salted fish and pig blood.

What with the swimming and the jogging, the morning section of my Thai routine was getting me in pretty decent shape. Around noon, when Devika woke up, she'd invariably want to start the day with a bang, as it were—and that just added to the workout. So until midafternoon I was the picture of healthy living.

At around four or five, however, Devika would magically produce a bottle of some kind of new and perverse Asian alcohol and the aforementioned craziness would ensue anew. That girl could drink! I told her on several occasions that she should visit Dublin. I knew of a variety of bars that would probably sponsor her trip and even pay for her hotel room, the way Vegas casinos do with high-stakes gamblers. She claimed that this was the way everyone in India drank but that can't possibly be true or how would they ever have been able to complete the Taj Mahal?

Devika usually picked out a destination for the evening's debauchery. Sometimes it was a bar in town. Sometimes it was a party in a nearby village. Sometimes it was an all-night rave at an abandoned train station. The key to every one of these activities was early and consistently maintained inebriation. Devika and I really didn't talk much. We would drink, have sex, drink some more, hang out with other people who were drinking while incredibly loud music was playing, then go back to my bungalow for a nightcap and some more sex.

I can't honestly say that I missed the opportunity to talk with her. One morning I woke up after having a weird dream. I was very hazy about what exactly had happened in it, but it was about my ex-wife and it left me feeling really unsettled. I woke Devika up from her fermented mare's milk–induced stupor and tried to tell her about it. But she was completely disinterested and fell back asleep almost immediately.

I remember feeling disappointed. I wasn't disappointed in Devika—after all, I could hardly expect this vivacious young wild woman to want to get bogged down in a morbid discussion about my failed marriage. It was more a diffuse sense of disappointment in myself. It wasn't a big deal, though, because a moment later the sheets slipped off Devika's sleeping body revealing one beautiful brown butt cheek and all thoughts of my ex-wife instantly vanished in a happy haze of horniness.

So we didn't talk. Who cares? Trust me, I'm not complaining. I had a young, exotic, sexy sex machine from the subcontinent enthusiastically coupling with me at every opportunity while I luxuriated in a magical oceanfront resort. If you complain about that, you deserve to get punched in the neck. I was cognizant of the fact that I had fallen into one of the great routines of all time and I had no interest in rocking the boat.

30

The boat got rocked for me, both literally and figuratively, about halfway through my stay in Thailand. I got a text message from Peter, my newly acquired LA writer friend who was staying in Phuket. He knew that I was in Krabi and was heading down that way on a private yacht. He wanted to know if I wanted to get together shipboard for some drinks and a quick cruise. It seemed like an amusing change of scenery. When I mentioned the idea to Devika she was interested. When I named the sitcoms that Peter created, she practically went insane. They're the kinds of shows that are always, at every second of every day, playing in syndication on some remote channel somewhere around the world. Apparently they had been huge hits in India. Sari-wearing Punjabis named their children after the main characters. She was thrilled and it was a done deal.

While there was no explicit rule against it, everyone at the Cove knew better than to reveal its location to outsiders. So

I agreed to meet Peter at the port in Laem Kruat where the ferries shuttle tourists back and forth from the islands. Chula took Devika and me to Laem Kruat and waited around to make sure that we actually met up with our friend and were not abducted by slavers, pirates, or Mormon missionaries. He nudged me frequently and winked lasciviously in reference to Devika. Chula was particularly pleased to see that I was engaged in an amorous adventure or, as he so quaintly put it, "making tok-tok." Seeing as how I happened to know that Chula had a doctorate in linguistics from the University of Sydney, I assumed that he was only speaking like that to make my Thai experience feel more authentic. And I appreciated it. There's nothing more satisfying than developing a warm relationship with an uneducated but streetwise native with a heart of gold—even if he is secretly a genius and is just perpetuating a stereotype to promote tourism.

Peter's yacht cruised into view. It was unmistakable. First off—it was the largest, glossiest, and snazziest-looking boat in the harbor. Granted, this was not a difficult feat to accomplish considering that most of the other boats were either wooden fishing vessels or rusty old ferries. But Peter's boat would have stood out in the harbors of Monaco, South Beach, or Newport, Rhode Island. Adnan Kashoggi would have been jealous of it. It had a helicopter pad on it—with an actual helicopter. As far as I'm concerned, you should either go yachting or go helicoptering. To do both simultaneously is just tacky.

And, speaking of tacky, another reason that Peter's boat stood out in the harbor is that the deck was filled with curvaceous young lovelies—only some of whom bothered wearing their skimpy bikinis. Chula and the native Thai fishermen setting their nets before heading out to sea stared at the arriving depravity with looks that spoke volumes. I don't know how to say, "I wish I was that guy" in Thai, but I now know exactly what that sentiment looks like.

Chula took off after a few more nudges and winks. Peter's boat tied up at harbor and Devika and I climbed aboard. The level of luxury on this ship was preposterous. It was an explosion of highly polished wood, more highly polished crystal, and hyperpolished gold. There was a crew member whose full-time job was to carve sexually suggestive ice sculptures. I should point out that all of the crew were female—and scantily clad in appropriately white-and-blue-striped nautical bikinis.

Every liquor known to man—and a few that might previously have been known only to apes and extraterrestrials—were on tap at any one of the seven—seven!—bars on board. The women were as artfully carved and as sexually suggestive as the ice sculptures. They also seemed to really enjoy the taste of coconut lip gloss because they were all constantly making out with each other.

To her credit, Devika fit right in. She was slamming Sangsom shots and triple-kissing Hooters girls faster than you can say *Girls Gone Wild*. The whole scene was wall-to-wall women at accelerated levels of undress and inebriation. Peter and I were clearly the only men on the boat. And Peter knew just what to do with his alpha-male status. He was busy licking salt off of the stomach of a bevy of hotties and then slurping little pools of tequila out of their belly buttons. The atmosphere was positively pornographic—and I actually mean that in a good way. Devika was grinding in between two half-naked models and beckoning me to join them with a seductively cocked—if you'll pardon the expression—finger.

So there I stood on deck of a truly phantasmagorical yacht watching as my nubile young lady friend invited me to engage in what would be—at a bare minimum—a threesome. I had never previously engaged in a threesome, nor had I seri-ously considered the possibility of one ever arising in my life. The closest I figured I'd ever get to a threesome would be if I pleasured myself using both hands. But here it was—not just a possibility but an inevitability. I was smack dab in the middle of Bonerville, ladies and gentlemen, and I was loving it.

As I shambled forward like a mental patient in search of mood stabilizers, I remember thinking to myself that this was it. This was the culmination of my yearlong voyage into the dark, secret heart of fun. I was about to become one of "those guys." You know who "those guys" are. They're the ones who party like rock stars and screw like porn stars. The guys who don't give a damn about anything more than keeping the good times going. And just one look at guys like that—and guys like I was about to become in a second—and you know that the good times are going to keep on going forever.

And I would have become one of "those guys." Really, I would have. There is no doubt in my mind that, if I hadn't glanced back for a second when I noticed that the yacht was finally pulling away from its moorings with a gentle lurch, I would have blindly and blissfully entered into that seething mass of female flesh and lost myself in ecstasy for all eternity.

But I did look back. It was an involuntary reaction. I felt the boat move. I heard one of the female crew members start to pull the gangplank back onto the deck, and I looked back for a moment.

That's when I spotted Alicia, the documentary filmmaker I met on Ireland's Whiskey Trail. When I suddenly saw her in the midst of the crowded dock at Laem Kruat, I realized that I'd been thinking about her ever since I'd left her at the Jameson castle in Midleton. And as soon as I saw her, things started getting a little weird.

31

The fact that I even noticed her was somewhat amazing. Between the insanity transpiring on board and the bustle of activity throughout the harbor, my view was a constantly moving blur of female flesh, short Thai men, bobbing boats, and lots of dead fish. But I noticed her right away. She was getting off a ferry along with her documentary crew. I even spotted the long fuzzy microphone thing.

It was definitely surprising that I picked her out of the crowd. I'd only met her that one time in Midleton when we'd walked and talked for a few hours. A few hours—big deal. I have, in the past, been known to fail to recognize old college roommates. And we spent months together. Granted, most of my college memories have transmogrified themselves into a haze of beer, melted butter, and burned popcorn. But, still—that had to mean something, right? I needed to be reintroduced to a guy with whom I spent all of 1991 and yet I instantly remembered a girl whom I only vaguely knew and who was

around 150 feet away from me surrounded by tourists, jabbering Asian fishermen, and recording equipment.

What was even more surprising than my noticing Alicia was
the feeling that suddenly washed over me the second I saw
her. Peter's boat was just pulling away from the pier and, as
the distance to the dock increased, I felt like a massive canyon
was opening in front of me that was about to swallow me up.
That warmth and camaraderie and connection that I had felt
when Alicia and I first met suddenly flashed through me, and
it was like I was feeling it for the first time all over again.

I took a step toward the edge of the boat and I heard Peter
call out from behind me.

"Watch out, Bobby!"

That snapped me out of my trance for a moment. I turned
around to see Peter looking up at me. His chin was nestled on
the stomach of an utterly naked redhead whose well-defined
abs were marked with steaks of salt and tequila.

"Careful where you step, buddy," Peter continued. "We
wouldn't want to lose you before the fun got started."

Behind Peter, Devika was still dancing with the two beautiful women. Her eyes were closed and she was completely
lost in the music and the drinking and the party. The beat of
whatever they were playing through the yacht's dozen hidden speakers was pumping. I could feel the bass pounding up
into my body through the deck. I looked back at the harbor
as it slowly became smaller and I saw that Alicia was looking
around for someone. Defying the remotest shred of possibility, I thought that maybe she was looking for me.

I felt like I was being teased by the gods. Behind me was a
hedonistic display of orgiastic excess the likes of which I had
never known before. It's entirely possible that no one on the
planet had ever known of the kind of wildness that was about

to go down on Peter's boat before. The whole scene had the kind of vibe that could only be created if an NBA star, a coked-to-the-gills record executive, the head of a major modeling agency, Larry Flynt, and Errol Flynn somehow chartered a yacht together and threw a naughty shindig. And what are the odds of that ever happening?

My brain knew that the next few hours on this boat would be mind-blowingly amazing. The kind of fun that fun seekers everywhere would whisper about in hushed tones referring to it as the legendary apotheosis of fun that occurred for one brief shining moment in the gulf of Thailand and was never to be repeated (or even approached) again.

But my heart kept making my eyeballs stare at that receding female figure in the harbor. What the hell was my heart thinking, my brain wanted to know. We could always play out this yacht thing for a while and track down Alicia later, right?

But my heart was not in a negotiating mood.

I used to be able to count on my brain rising up and kicking my heart's ass whenever things got dicey. Back in my old life, my brain ruled the roost. Sure, my heart wanted to watch the final nine holes of the Masters. But my brain knew that there would be hell to pay if we didn't do what my wife wanted. So my heart backed down and we went to a poetry reading, or someone's wedding, or I repainted the laundry room. To this day I can't watch replays of Phil Mickelson's first win at Augusta without wincing. And it's not just because that little victory leap he took with the nerdy fist pump was so embarrassing.

I assumed that my brain would kick my heart's ass this time too. But apparently my heart had been working out during my year of traveling. Or maybe my brain had just gotten really weak with all the drinking, gambling, and screwing. But the next thing I knew, my heart got in touch with my feet and suddenly my feet, my heart, and all the rest of me were running across the yacht's deck toward the edge. I heard Peter yell, "Bobby! What the fuck?!" And then I was leaping over the edge into the water.

Fortunately my heart also communicated with my arms and had them start paddling toward the harbor. My brain was extremely surprised. Not quite as surprised as Peter, however. I heard him yelling at me from the yacht.

"Are you out of your fucking mind?!"

I turned back to him as I swam.

"Sorry, Peter! I have to see someone! Bye!"

Peter watched me swim away with a look of confusion and a little bit of disgust.

"Yeah, whatever," he replied. "Just watch out for those little fish that swim up your dick!"

And those were the last words I ever heard him say. Not necessarily the most momentous of farewells. But, then again, he wasn't the most momentous of guys. Considering that I met Peter at an airport as well, I might have expected him to have a more profound effect on me like Colin and Rick did. But I guess not everyone you meet in an airport can be your guru. Or maybe you can meet your gurus only at the baggage claim.

Anyway, my heart, feet, arms, legs, eyeballs, ear sockets, and islets of Langerhans were all regretting my decision to jump and swim pretty quickly. My clothes were weighing me down and the possibility of penis fish—no matter how unlikely—was disturbing. Luckily, the dock wasn't far away and before long I was pulling myself out of the water to the great amusement of dozens of Thai fishermen. All in all, this had been an extremely entertaining morning for them.

I ran up the ramp that led to the pier. Then I ran down the pier toward the area where Alicia had emerged from the ferry. The port was really crowded so I had to pick my way through the tourists and locals and even some livestock. I debated whether or not I should shout out "Alicia!" My first instinct was that it would be way too clichéd and melodramatic to do that. Although I really liked it when Rocky called for Adrienne at the end of *Rocky*. But they had a relationship already and it felt more organic. Just like they teach you when you take the SATs, I went with my first instinct and kept quiet.

By the time I got to the ferry landing, however, I immediately wished that I had pulled a Rocky and shouted out Alicia's name. Because she was nowhere in sight.

So there I stood: dripping wet, out of breath, perplexed, and slightly stunned. In the distance I heard the unmistakable sound of a ship's horn. I looked out to sea just in time to spot Peter's yacht cruising around a bend and disappearing from sight.

I have often suspected that I am an idiot but my suspicions have rarely been confirmed to the degree that they were at that moment. Soaked, stupid, sad, and alone I started trudging my way back to the Cove.

32

I have no idea what I had hoped to achieve with my reckless dive from Peter's yacht and subsequent Australian crawl back to shore. I guess I was planning on some kind of Hollywood-y romantic reunion drama. Like Alicia would see me all wet and crazy and she'd instantly realize that we were soul mates and we'd kiss and hug and then she'd get some laughs complaining that I was ruining her new outfit. Then I'd undercut the laughs by saying something like, "We've got the rest of our lives to get you a new outfit." Then the credits would roll and the audience would sniffle and smile and head out of the theater blinking into the sunlight and wondering why their lives sucked so bad.

That's not what happened. Instead I ended up taking a rickety bus filled with old women and chickens as close to the Cove as I could get. Then I hired an eight-year-old boy to row me across the lagoon. He spoke English well enough to radically overcharge me for the trip. I never quite figured out the baht-to-dollar exchange rate, but I think I paid him around $300. In order to preserve the secret sanctity of the Cove, I told the kid an elaborate lie that I was an avid bird-watcher and there had been a recent sighting of a rare Nicobar pigeon across the lagoon. The kid just shrugged and said he figured that I was going to the Cove, but good luck with the birds. It turned out that the Cove was primarily a secret for the Western world. Most Thai locals were very much aware of the resort—they just didn't care about it.

The kid left me on the far side of the lagoon and, as soon as he was gone, I wished that he—or some other Thai local—would come back. Because those guys might know all about the Cove's whereabouts but I was damned if I could remember how to get there. The whole coastline was dense jungle. I had passed through here several times in the 4x4 with Chula, but I didn't see a single opening in the flora large enough for Kate Moss to pass through, let alone a truck.

I thought I saw a path so I pushed through the foliage into the jungle. After approximately eight seconds of thrashing about through the bush, I was completely lost. There was no path. I was unable to retrace my steps back to the beach. Every step I did take seemed to lead me deeper and deeper into the bowels of the wild.

It was now about eight hundred degrees. Flies were eating me alive. Scary jungle noises were emanating from, appropriately, the jungle. The overgrowth was so thick that I couldn't even see the sun through the trees. I had no water, no food, I had humiliated myself in front of Devika (who I had also abandoned), and I was utterly convinced that I was never going to see Alicia again.

I sat down in a small opening between two banana trees and I buried my head in my hands. I probably should have cried,

but it just didn't happen. I hope that doesn't mitigate my de-
pression. I mean, lots of people cry for no reason—that doesn't
mean they're sadder than they really are. So take my word for
it—I was sad. I'm talking sad on an existential level. It was as
if all the wonderful times that I'd had all year were suddenly
meaningless—and I couldn't figure out why.

I knew that I had an awesome adventure. Ireland, Vegas,
Thailand . . . I'd seen things and met people and had experiences that I never could have imagined in my old life. So
why was I sitting in the woods, lost and scared and upset?
Could it really be Alicia? Was I just so pathetic that I couldn't
stand to be alone? Or was there something special about her?
Was she really the one for me? And had I recognized that
fact just a hair too late, and now I was never going to know
for sure?

What kind of an idiot loser sits in the tropical jungle and
asks himself nothing but whiny, unanswerable questions? Because they were unanswerable. The only way I'd ever be able
to know the truth—the only way I'd ever find out if Alicia
was the key to my deep, true, and everlasting happiness—
would be if she were with me at that moment. And that was
impossible. So I should just forget about her and get on with
my idiot loser life—which might be over soon anyway if I
couldn't find my way out of here.

I stood up, took one step between the two banana trees,
and instantly got hit by a speeding SUV.

Technically speaking, it was the 4x4 driven by Chula—but
that's still an SUV, right? I've never been clear on that subject. Can you call one of those old-school, open-top Jeeps an
SUV? Is that the one thing that Dwight D. Eisenhower has in
common with a soccer mom? Or is a Jeep a Jeep and I should
shut up already? I guess I'll never know.

What I did know was that I had obviously stumbled across the path through the jungle to the Cove and that Chula had just nailed me with the company 4x4. I knew that Chula was driving because, after the truck hit me, I bounced up over the fender and landed on the hood, staring right through the windshield. So I could clearly see Chula's face, which was frozen in horror and surprise.

I was even more surprised than Chula, however. Because not only had a vehicle just crashed into me out of the blue in the middle of the jungle while I was bemoaning the fact that I'd never see Alicia again—but Alicia was sitting in the passenger seat.

33

Okay—it's an extremely unlikely turn of events. I know this. The serendipitous nature of this accident strains credulity. But I really would like you to believe me. It happened. Hell, bizarre things happen all the time. Once I was walking past a Starbucks in Phoenix and I suddenly decided to call an old college friend whom I hadn't seen in years. When he answered the phone, it turned out that he was sitting in the exact same Starbucks that I was walking past! God (and/or the universe) works in mysterious ways. (An interesting footnote to that story: when I went into the Starbucks to see my friend, Sean Astin was sitting there drinking a frappuccino. You know, Sean Astin the actor. Samwise Gamgee from the *Lord of the Rings* trilogy, just chilling out with some java. He was in town for a book signing tour. I was so excited to see him that I actually forgot that my college friend was there.)

There were no hobbits, elves, or wizards in the 4x4. But I don't think I would have been any more shocked if there had been. Alicia was totally stunned as well. I'm pretty sure that all three of us were screaming in fear and surprise. After a few seconds—and, frankly, a few seconds too many—Chula slammed on the brakes. I flew off the hood, smashed into a mahogany tree, and landed in a thicket of ginger plants.

When I looked up, Alicia was standing over me. Her mouth was moving but all I could hear was the blood rushing in my head. I don't know if it was love or a severe concussion, but I just stared at her without understanding a word she said. She knelt down beside me and laid her hand against my forehead. Somehow, even in the horrible heat, her skin was cool and soothing. Her touch rescued me from my stupor and I could understand her now.

"Bobby? Are you okay?" she asked.

Bobby. She remembered my name. An excellent sign. I explained that—considering I had just been struck by a vehicle—I actually felt fine. And I really did. I felt great. I asked her what she was doing here. Her response was, "What am *I* doing here? What are *you* doing here?"

I was about to answer her as she and Chula helped me to my feet but I got sidetracked by the most profound agony that I had ever experienced. I shrieked like a wounded schoolgirl (not my finest hour) and collapsed to the ground, shuddering. My entire pelvic region had suddenly turned into a giant ball of pain. It felt like the area between my hip bones was filled with liquid fire and shattered glass. This is not a good feeling.

"We have to get him to a hospital," Alicia said. I agreed wholeheartedly.

But Chula had a different plan. He explained that the Thai countryside was a place of great beauty and spirituality. It was also a place of terrible health care. His uncle Panyarachun went to the local hospital once complaining of shortness of breath.

One of the doctors removed his liver and sold it on the Laotian black market. I quickly shifted my wholehearted agreement to the "no hospital" camp.

Chula told us that, without a doubt, the best medical care possible would be found at the Cove. Since everything else there was first class I assumed that he was right about this too. So he and Alicia lifted me up and placed me in the back of the truck as carefully as they could, which was no way nearly careful enough. We drove back to the Cove at around two miles per hour—but the uneven jungle path and the fifty-year-old shock absorbers were not doing my damaged body any favors.

Alicia held my hand and tried to distract me from the pain by commenting on the sights.

"Look," she said, pointing off into the greenery. "Isn't that a long-tailed macaque?" Chula nailed a massive pothole and, for a moment, I saw nothing but white light and I thought that my heart was going to pop out of my chest like the baby monster in *Alien*. Alicia squeezed my hand, pointed to another sliver of jungle canopy, and said, "I'm pretty sure that's a red-necked phalarope."

I was not interested in the native wildlife. But I appreciated the effort. I squeezed her hand in return. I was aware that I was in some serious physical pain. But I truly and honestly didn't care, because I was holding hands with Alicia while she insisted on naming every frigging animal she saw in the jungle. I guess my unanswerable questions were being answered after all. A moment ago I was miserable. Now Alicia was here and I was happy.

For all of God's (and/or the universe's) mysterious ways, sometimes things are extremely simple. You can talk and talk and pray and pray and meditate and meditate, but none of that will change the facts of life. And one of those facts is as follows. Even when you're scared, lost, overheated, lonely, miserable, and in extreme agony after having been struck in the midsection by an automobile, the right woman can magically make everything instantly okay.

34

I must have passed out at some point during the drive because the next thing I remember is waking up in a large, comfortable bed in a beautifully appointed bungalow while the sound of waves slapping against the sand floated in through the windows and a ceiling fan gently caressed sweet breezes throughout the room. A lovely young Thai woman in a nurse's uniform was applying a cold compress to my forehead. You know how in the movies people wake up in these idyllic situations and think that they're dead? Well, I actively wished that I were dead and in heaven. All I needed was a sixty-inch HDTV with a satellite hookup and I was set for all eternity. But as I shifted slightly in bed, the lightning bolt of pain that shot through my body shattered my fantasy. It seems unlikely that one would have tear-inducing discomfort in heaven. That kind of ruins the whole idea of paradise—even if there are hot Asian nurses.

I have never been one to suffer quietly and I think that I may have let loose with another ear-splitting little-girl scream.

Alicia ran into the room and I attempted to toughen up. As soon as I saw her I remembered why I was glad that I wasn't dead. Sexy angel nurses are fine—but they're really nothing more than a nice appetizer. Alicia was a full meal—with a rich Chianti and some crème brûlée thrown in for good measure.

She explained to me that I had been unconscious for almost twenty-four hours—partly due to the massive amounts of pain medicine that had been administered intravenously. As luck would have it, the head orthopedist from Oklahoma Surgical Hospital was staying at the Cove. She had already diagnosed me with a slightly fractured pelvis and prescribed extended bed rest and the continued liberal intake of pain meds. I didn't really need the head orthopedist from Oklahoma Surgical Hospital to tell me to stay in bed. I wasn't physically capable of going anywhere anyway. Fortunately the beautifully appointed room I was in turned out to actually be my bedroom in my bungalow. Alicia and Chula had carried me all the way there while I was out cold. So all the moving that I was going to do had been done for me already.

Alicia explained to me that she was at the Cove to film it as part of her documentary about great, underexposed travel destinations. When I pointed out that the Cove wasn't so much underexposed as it was a total secret, she said that she would be maintaining the site's anonymity. I was wondering how she even knew about the Cove but that question temporarily got lost among the other million questions I had for her. I wanted to know what she'd been up to since Ireland, and she was interested in the same about me. But first she had to check in with her film crew and get them set up to start shooting. She headed off but promised to come back in a few hours.

As I watched her go I actually sighed out loud. That may not sound like that big a deal—but how often do you actually sigh audibly? Think about it. Not that often, I bet. I heard the sound I'd just made and it startled me. What the hell was going on here? Shrieking, fainting, sighing . . . I was starting to act like a character from a Jane Austen novel. Either I was in love or I was Elinor Dashwood.

Before I get into the whole Alicia thing too deeply—and it's gonna get deep, brace yourselves—let me say a few things about a broken pelvis. It sucks. That's just one thing to say, I guess, but it's the only thing that needs to be said. Frankly, I was extremely lucky to have sustained only a mild fracture. Had Chula whacked me a little bit harder, or if I'd ricocheted off that mahogany tree with a little more force, the bones might have snapped clean through. And then I'd be in the middle of a whole other kind of nightmare. As it was, I felt pretty comfortable as long as I didn't move or put pressure on it. Dr. Oklahoma assured me that if I just took it easy and allowed the crack to heal, I'd be fine and dandy within a month. The bedpan issue was the most unpleasant part of the whole situation and I am definitely not going to get into that in any kind of graphic detail. Suffice it to say that the hot Asian nurse—whose name was Maliwan and turned out to be so unbelievably sweet that I felt terrible about ever having thought of her as a hot Asian nurse—truly was an angel. Tipping was forbidden at the Cove, but before I left I bought Maliwan a Vespa. Trust me—she earned it.

So there I was in my bed, immobilized by a fissure in my pelvic bone. And as painful as the prospect of moving even a centimeter was to me, I would rather have done a dozen jumping jacks on a trampoline while a motorcycle gang kicked me in the groin than do what I had to do next. But sometimes a guy's gotta do what a guy's gotta do. I took advantage of Alicia's temporary absence and asked Chula to see if Devika would come by.

35

I heard the footsteps outside my room before I saw her enter.
I prepared myself for drama. I have not had a ton of experience dealing with different women in my life. My wife is the
primary point of reference when it comes to anticipating how
women will react. If I had abandoned my wife on a boat surrounded by strangers and swam away looking for another
woman, I'm pretty sure how she would respond. She would
go apeshit—not that I can really blame her. Getting ditched
in the Gulf of Thailand is right up there with being left behind at the circus when your parents take you into the city to
see the elephants. In their defense, they did come right back
as soon as they realized their mistake. Plus it was a simpler time
back then before all the Internet predators and such. Anyway,
as angry as I was at my folks, I figured that Devika would be
even more pissed off at me.

She entered the room and right away I saw that I had it all
wrong. She wasn't mad. She was concerned. She thought that

I'd fallen off the boat and broken my pelvis when I hit the water. So, now, not only did I have to apologize for abandoning her, I had to explain to her that I abandoned her and *then* apologize for it.

I easily could have let her believe her version of the story, but I wanted to be honest with her. Small lies turn into big lies, which turn into weeping and name-calling and throwing a stapler at my framed, autographed Don Mattingly jersey. I was going to come clean. I started telling Devika about my ex-wife and about Alicia but she cut me off.

"Bobby, please. You don't have to explain anything to me. I made you feel good. You made me feel good. Now we're moving on. No big deal."

I couldn't believe it. "You're really not mad?" I asked.

"How can I be mad?" she answered. "I was so busy drinking, dancing, and banging strangers that I didn't even notice you weren't there until the boat landed this morning."

That certainly took the sting out of my betrayal. I told her that she was a great kid and an excellent ambassador for India. I had always assumed that her country was a bastion of backward-thinking traditionalism. Now I've learned that the whole place is filled with fun-loving, sexually adventurous party girls who drink like sailors on shore leave. That's a much more pleasant assumption, and one that's guaranteed to boost tourism.

Devika told me not to worry. She wouldn't interfere with whatever I had going with Alicia. Besides, she was leaving in a few days to join her parents in Cambodia and then head back to Japan. I thanked her from the bottom of my heart. She really had helped me rediscover a whole side to life that I had almost forgotten about. I tried to hug her good-bye but it hurt my groinal area so badly that I just settled for a heartfelt fist bump.

Devika kissed me on the forehead and left. I have not seen her again since then but I wish her well every day. She's a good person, and she's going to make some guy (or possibly several guys, and maybe even a few girls) very, very happy.

Later that afternoon Alicia came back. She told me that her crew was shooting B-roll around the property. I nodded sagely and acted like I knew what B-roll was. She realized that I was full of shit and explained that B-roll was footage of secondary importance that would be edited into the main body of the movie as cutaways. Her point was that she wasn't needed on set while they were filming so we finally had some time to talk.

At first I didn't know what to say. We both kind of sputtered and stammered and hemmed and hawed until I got things going with stories about Las Vegas. Then she'd jump in with anecdotes from the places she'd seen while researching her documentary. We'd go back and forth with weird hotel stories or travel nightmares or descriptions of lunatics we'd met along the way.

I was trying my hardest not to laugh but the lady cracked me up, which hurt like a bastard. She asked if I wanted her to leave so that I could rest. I definitely did not. I told her to keep on being funny and I'd just increase the dosage of my morphine drip.

We sat there for hours until it was pitch black outside and all we could hear was the sound of the ocean and the rustle and screech of jungle animals prowling at night. Alicia had been so preoccupied with getting her film crew going and then talking to me that she hadn't even checked into her room. I graciously offered to let her crash next to me on the world's largest, most comfortable bed. Just until the next morning when she could get into her room.

"You have nothing to worry about," I added. "It would be physically impossible for me to try any moves on you without bursting into tears first and begging for my mommy."

"Wow," she shot back. "You really know what turns me on. Have you been reading my Facebook page?"

The woman made jokes about sexual perversion and Hitler hiring an assistant director. Some people might find that inappropriate. Good for them. As for me, I laughed so hard that not even the morphine could dull the pain. And then Alicia climbed into bed next to me and fell asleep holding my hand.

One of the drawbacks of a broken pelvis—aside form the shooting pain, the inability to go to the bathroom on your own, and the complete cessation of any kind of a sex life—is that you have to sleep on your back. "Big deal," you might say. "I sleep on my back all the time." Uh . . . no you don't. You might think you do, but as soon as you're asleep, you're rolling around like Burt Lancaster on a Hawaiian beach. I, on the other hand, could only lie on my back. So sleep was hard to achieve and it was intermittent.

Normally there's nothing as irksome as lousy, fitful sleep. But it's not so bad when you're sleeping lousily and fitfully next to the right person. I'd say I spent at least half that night wide awake staring at Alicia's face in the moonlight. I found it to be almost preternaturally soothing. It's not just that it is a beautiful face. It is—at least I think so. But on some very profound level I felt that it was the right face for me.

Did I ever think that my wife's face was "the right face for me"? An excellent question. And the answer is that I certainly never thought that her face was wrong for me. I just never thought about it. In eight years of marriage (and a few years of dating before that), there was never a moment where it all just clicked into place and I realized it was the right fit. I liked her—

I loved her—and I really wanted us to fit together. But just because you want something, and you work hard to make it happen, doesn't mean that it's right.

Staring at Alicia's face I had no way of knowing what the future would hold in store for us. But I knew that I wanted to find out. I knew that this was something that was worth pursuing. And at that moment I felt a real sense of appreciation for my wife and everything that she had put me through. It wasn't just that the divorce inadvertently led me to meeting Alicia. It was that the journey from New York to Ireland to Las Vegas to Thailand had changed me. I was different than I was before. I'm not going to say that I was better now. But the changes allowed me to realize that Alicia was someone special and that was enough for me. That felt about as good as anything could feel. And I wasn't going to let this one go (assuming that she felt something similar—and I was pretty sure she did seeing as how she was asleep in my bed holding my hand).

Fortunately I finally fell asleep for good before I composed a frigging sonnet for her. When I woke up she wasn't lying next to me and I had a moment of sheer panic. Was it all a dream? Had she actually been there but came to her senses and fled the country? Was I really dead after all but this wasn't heaven—it was hell?

Two seconds later, Alicia came in carrying a tray of fresh-cut papaya and a pitcher of mango juice. It was heaven.

36

There's one more wrinkle to my history with Alicia. I didn't find it out until she'd been in Thailand for a few weeks. She and her film crew were meeting in my bungalow and they were going over the shot list for the day. They wanted an impressive establishing shot of the lagoon and I suggested that they climb a little hill about fifty yards behind the main building and shoot down onto the property from there. They were all pleased with the suggestion and headed out to set up. It struck me again that the Cove was an odd place for Alicia and her crew to have chosen. None of them knew anything about it. Even if she had agreed to preserve the secrecy of its location, how had she found out about it to begin with?

Alicia explained that I was right—she had never heard of the Cove in her life. But she was filming a segment of her documentary at a little-known but world-class bonefishing hotel in the Bahamas when she struck up a conversation with a guest there. When he found out what she was doing, he told her all about the Cove. Then he offered to make some calls and he got her in.

It all made sense and I wouldn't have thought any more about it if she hadn't gone on to say the following: "He was an amazing guy. Really smart and really nice. The only weird thing about him was that he showed up for a six-week stay in the Caribbean with nothing but a set of golf clubs."

"Hold it," I said. "What's his name?"

What do you think she said? Of course—it was Rick. We double-checked personal details. It was the same guy. Her Rick was my Rick. That's right, people. Talk about preposterous serendipity. Rick bumped into the love of my life and then sent her to Thailand to make my dreams come true. Talk about a kick-ass guru . . . I owe that guy more than I could ever repay.

Alicia and I spent the next two months at the Cove. She never bothered checking into her room. I didn't leave my bed for the first three weeks and she was by my side every night. Our relationship grew slowly. It was obvious how we felt about each other but my delicate medical condition made it impossible for things to get too physical too soon. But that was fine. Actually, it was great. We really got to know each other before we, well, got to know each other.

And we did get to know each other, if you know what I'm talking about. Once again, I'm not getting into details here because I'm a semi-gentleman and this is the woman I love after all. But you may be happy to know that we fit together as well on a physical level as we did on all other levels. God knows that I was happy to know that. When I finally got medical clearance to get busy, we dedicated ourselves to making up for lost time.

And as good as the sex was with Devika, being with Alicia was something completely separate and apart. I have no interest in parsing the differences between fucking and making love. I leave that to the great poets as well as the mediocre rappers. All I know is that I love Alicia and that permeates everything I feel, think, and do.

Some people might think that I'm a sucker. I had a chance for an orgy with a gaggle of sexy porn chicks and I chose monogamy with a documentary filmmaker. Well, whatever. Let each of you face that choice and then see if you can live with the decision. I am blissfully happy with the option I went with and I have absolutely no regrets.

Alicia and I are still together. Sometimes we're both in LA. Sometimes we're both in New York. Sometimes we're apart. Sometimes we travel the world together. It doesn't really matter because we share a connection that time and space cannot sever. I realize that makes me sound like a spiritual goofball and I apologize. Nothing annoys me more than hearing the unwanted vocalization of someone else's special inner beliefs.

I like to keep things simple. Some people wonder how they're supposed to make it through each day with all the misery in the world. And I'm aware that the world can be a horrible place. I have no answer for the doubters and the naysayers. I'm not here to convince anyone of anything. All I know is that—yes, it's easy to be sad. But it's also easy to be happy. How are you supposed to be happy? I have no idea. I don't even know you. But here are a few things that make me happy.

1. A walk-off home run—preferably delivered by a New York Yankee.
2. Picking an apple off of a tree, eating it in about five bites, and throwing the core at the base of the tree.
3. Watching the back nine of Masters Sunday and *then* going to see the Guarneri String Quartet with Alicia.

4. Driving a convertible (as long as it has an automatic transmission).
5. Throwing a tennis ball to a dog and having him bring it right back to me and dropping it at my feet (and not having it be too slimy).
6. Seeing a stranger carry another stranger's stroller up the steps of the subway.
7. Riding a power mower across a large expanse of uncut grass.
8. Going to Madrid and eating twelve different types of tapas in twelve different bars in one night.
9. Flopping the nuts to win a poker tournament at Foxwoods.
10. Holding Alicia's hand.

Whenever I have a chance, I go back and revisit some of the places where I spent my year abroad. Sometimes Alicia comes with me. Sometimes I go alone. I've seen Colin several times. He got an Irish passport and is now leading tourists through the many sights, sounds, and tastes of Temple Bar. He told me that Giovanna got married to Teodoro and that they already have three kids. Mathematically this seems impossible unless at least two of them are twins.

The faces always change in Vegas but I still get comped to that supersuite whenever I go to the Bellagio. I make sure to blow enough money at the tables to maintain the rep and then I tip everyone like a gangster. Most of the time I meet up with Rick when I'm there. We get in a few rounds of golf and then we hit the sports book hard. We still play crazy trifectas although recently we've been working on an even crazier series of six-way parlays that we're trying to copyright as "sexfectas." There has not been a great deal of interest from anyone else on that front.

Alicia and I spent two weeks at the Cove recently. I hesitate to call it a honeymoon because that word has always sounded a little tacky to me. We did get married just before going there, however, so I guess calling it a honeymoon would be more accurate than tacky. I won't bore you with the wedding details. It was very nice. Rick was my best man. Everyone's family got along. There was plenty of drinking but no fighting. It was lovely.

We had a delightful reunion with Maliwan. She's still riding the Vespa I bought her and is now engaged to a local fisherman who actually remembered me from my dive off of Peter's boat. I haven't seen Peter since that morning in the harbor near Laem Kruat. I heard that he created a new sitcom about a horse barn but I don't know if it'll ever see the light of day.

Alicia and I were both disappointed to discover that Chula no longer works at the Cove. But we were pleased to discover that he is now the chairman of the linguistics department at Chulalongkorn University—otherwise known as the Harvard of Thailand. It's clearly a perfect fit, as it says "Chula" right there in the name of the school.

So that pretty much wraps up where everyone is these days. As for me, well . . . on the roulette wheel of life, I find myself happily bouncing along from number to number never knowing where I'll land, but content no matter where I end up. Alicia and I are together forever (fingers crossed) and life is good. As for my ex-wife, I wish her well. I hope she's not too upset with me for writing this book. Lord knows I'd be pissed off if she wrote one.

The End

I would like to thank the following people for their creativity, support, advice, and money: Rick Brenders, Paula Diaz-Reixa, Claire Dippel, Alicia Ezpeleta, Alexandra Gottlieb, Cristina Gottlieb, Lucas Janklow, Scott Manning, Colin O'Neill, Eric Price, Will Schwalbe, Jamison Stoltz, Martin Wilson, and Warner Bros.